# BUYING

# H

## A COMPREHENSIVE GUIDE TO PREPARING FOR, FINDING AND PURCHASING A GREAT HORSE

*Mary Guay*
*and*
*Donna Schlinkert*

**WHITE PAPERS PRESS**
**MARIETTA, GA**

# Buying Your First Horse

A Comprehensive Guide to Preparing for, Finding and
Purchasing a Great Horse

By Mary Guay
and
Donna Schlinkert

Copyright © 1997 by Mary Guay and Donna Schlinkert

Published by:
White Papers Press
Post Office Box 72294
Marietta, GA  30007-2294

Library of Congress Catalog Card Number:  96-61360

ISBN 0-9654669-6-5
Second Printing August 1998
Third Printing October 2000
Printed in Canada

# Acknowledgments

The authors wish to thank many people for their help and support in producing "Buying Your First Horse". To all the riders and boarders at West Haven Farm, thank you for providing a model equestrian community and appearing in the many pictures in this book.

Special thanks to Doug Purvis, Commercial Photography, Atlanta Georgia, for the cover photo and the lovely photos on pages 49, 57, 64, 68, 114 and 126. And many thanks to Diane Purvis for model preparation. It was a pleasure to work with you, and happy relic hunting!

Thanks to Jean Abernethy for the wonderful illustration on the cover page and at the end of each chapter.

Thank you to the authors of the other equestrian books referenced in the appendix for providing excellent background information.

And for encouragement, support and belief in us, we are grateful to our big, tight, fun family.

# About the Authors

Mary Guay and Donna Schlinkert are sisters who grew up with a love for horses starting with their first horse, Traveler. Mary, formerly in computer networking, is now a writer in Atlanta, Ga.

Donna is a lifelong professional equestrian who now owns and manages West Haven Farm in Dallas, Georgia, a successful boarding and training facility. She has over 20 years of international experience in the equestrian industry which includes training horses, training riders, showing, brokering horses, boarding horses and managing barns. She was educated at Meredith Manor in West Virginia. As a broker and trainer, Donna often is asked to find horses for riders who have no idea how to select and purchase a horse that is safe, fairly priced, sound and a great ride.

# CONTENTS

# SECTION ONE

# PREPARING FOR YOUR

# HORSE

BUYING YOUR FIRST HORSE

# INTRODUCTION

Y ou, or someone close to you, wants to own a horse. Congratulations - you are about to enter a wonderful sport that will provide a lifetime of fun and fulfillment. There is no other sport that is equally open to young and old, male and female regardless of size. Riding can be relaxing and exhilarating and enjoyed by the entire family. The equestrian community spans the spectrum of socioeconomic classes from the humblest country farm to the most elegant royal stable. Riding sports are diverse, including racing, trail riding, rodeos and Olympic competition. Though diverse, one aspect is shared by the entire equestrian community: the bond between horse and rider. Caring for your own horse can create a trusting, educational and emotional bond that can last a lifetime.

On a more practical note, how do you find that perfect horse? Will you pay a fair price? How can you increase your chances of finding a safe horse that doesn't bite, kick, rear or buck? Are you ready for the commitment? How do you avoid the unsound horse? Because this decision will affect you for years to come, you should prepare as thoroughly as possible. This book will help you answer these questions and more.

The issues in this guide relate to all riding disciplines - English (hunt seat, dressage, saddle seat or combined training) and Western (stock, roping, reining, or pleasure). Both horse buyer and rider, if not one in the same, will benefit from the information within.

It takes years of professional involvement with horses to adequately judge the potential of a horse. The information in this book will prepare you for horse ownership, and guide you in making the best choice. If you are a beginning rider, you should use this guide along with the help of your instructor to select your horse.

Buying a horse is a tremendous commitment and a long-term decision. A successful horse and rider have a strong, long term relationship. You can insure this by putting careful and deliberate thought into the selection of your horse. Horses vary widely in temperament, price, size and ability. Whether you are buying a horse for yourself, your child or someone else, you want to choose a horse that will match the rider's abilities and one that will be able to grow with the rider's skills. You want a horse that's safe and healthy, one without bad habits, and of course, you want to pay fair price. This guide will help you be better prepared and more confident that the horse that you purchase is safe, a good buy and a great ride.

The first section of the book deals with preparing for your horse. This is not meant to discourage you from your dream of owning a horse. Rather, it is meant to be a realistic look at all the issues of horse ownership and to help you avoid some pitfalls that may prevent you from thoroughly enjoying horse ownership. If you absorb these facts, fully understand what you are about to undertake, and still have that dream, then you are a true horse lover and will be even more anxious to become a horse owner.

# IF THE RIDER IS A CHILD

**M**any first time horse buyers are buying a horse or pony for their child. Children, especially young girls, can be completely enchanted with horses. For them, it is an emotional decision. For you, the decision should be based on solid information, and safety should be your first concern. If the rider is a very young child, then you will be ultimately responsible for the horse's care and your child's safety.

How young is too young to own a horse? Generally, a child of six years old is too young to understand or appreciate such a responsibility. No horse is completely safe around such a young child. Until about age 12, a child will need close guidance and supervision with the care of his horse, and the development of his riding skills. After age 12, many children will begin to develop a sense of commitment and responsibility. They will also be more able to handle the athletic demands of riding and horsecare, and respect safety guidelines. Of course, children develop and mature at different rates.

## IF THE RIDER IS A CHILD

Most children cannot be expected to anticipate the effort and commitment required in caring for a horse. You, as a parent, will take on this responsibility until your child has matured enough to do so. Even a child as old as 15 can have little insight into the reality of dealing with a horse on a daily basis.

If you are buying this horse for someone else's child be certain that his or her parents are fully aware of all the responsibilities that are inherent with horse ownership. Certainly, a surprise gift of a horse to someone else's child can create many dilemmas. You may absolutely delight the child, but the parents may not be willing or able to pay for its continued care, and they may not even want their child involved in equestrian activity for one reason or another. The parents are then put in the position of breaking their child's heart.

For the child or adult that truly loves horses, owning and caring for a horse can be a terrific learning experience and self esteem booster. Horse ownership is a large commitment, and this responsibility turns into reward for the owner by:

- Realizing the responsibility of a daily commitment

- Developing an athletic activity that can last a lifetime

- Learning sportsmanship in competition

- Developing both a student and teacher relationship with a horse that is based on trust

- Seeing the efforts of quality care, preparation and practice result in great performance and successful competition

You may wish to consider leasing a horse for your child for a year (for all 4 seasons) prior to purchasing one. Caring for a horse through the winter while in school can be quite different than the summer months. If dedicated and serious, your child can progress in a years time and you will have a much better indication of what type of horse is the best match, and whether the child is still anxious to devote all the time necessary to maintaining the sport and the animal. See the chapter on "Leasing a Horse".

# SAFETY

R iding and caring for a horse need not be dangerous. If you are a parent of the rider, you may have concerns about safety. The great majority of injuries that occur with horses can be prevented or reduced by being informed and attentive. You can reduce the risk considerably by following certain guidelines:

• Always wear headgear approved by the American Horse Show Association while riding and handling horses. This should be a rule and a habit, much like wearing a seat belt. Headgear can significantly reduce serious injury and chance of death. Headgear is important not only while riding to reduce injury from a fall, but also while handling horses to reduce injury from kicking.

It is currently not "in fashion" for Western riders to wear protective headgear even though Western riding is just as dangerous as English. Western riders as well as English riders should always wear headgear.

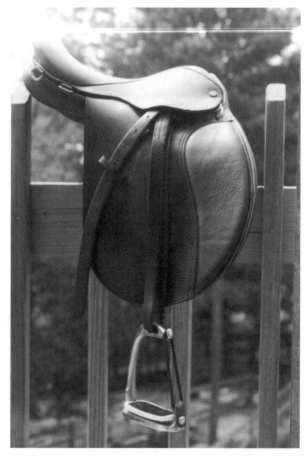

*Breakaway stirrups on an English saddle.*

• Buy tack that has safety features such as break away stirrups (English) or toe guards (Western). With these stirrups, the rider's foot will not get stuck in the stirrup if thrown. Other stirrups can allow the foot to go completely through and if the rider is thrown he could be dragged or trampled.

• Wear leather riding shoes or boots to prevent injury to feet and toes if stepped on. Proper shoes will also keep your foot in the stirrup more securely.

• Be sure all tack is properly cared for and examined before using, so that straps and buckles don't break unexpectedly. Most tack is leather, and if left out in the elements, not cleaned and conditioned, can become brittle. Leather loses elasticity and can break or pinch and irritate the horse. Horses can buck, kick, bite or rear to relieve themselves of irritating tack. A break on a bridle strap or rein can result in loss of control.

• Take lessons regularly. Your instructor can spot potential accidents before they happen and prevent you and your horse from establishing bad habits.

• Ride in safe areas which are designated for horses such as trails and arenas. Avoid congested areas and roads. Few horses can tolerate cars speeding by, and some drivers will actually honk or throw an object at a rider and horse as they speed by.

- When trail riding, avoid untested pastures or woods where holes or obstructions may cause your horse to trip or fall. If you want to establish a trail in a new area, walk the untried trail without your horse first, cutting away irritating branches and checking for ruts. Mark a specific trail. Check your parks service for parks that have horse trails. Even if you are riding on an established riding trail, be cautious on your first ride so that you and your horse get to know the terrain and obstacles. Also, keep a safe distance before and after each horse to avoid biting, bucking and kicking.

- Know your limitations and your horse's limitations. Don't jump until you've had solid training and be sure your trainer is with you. Don't ask your horse to jump a fence that he may refuse.

- Know your horse's peculiarities, such as spooking at water crossings or certain objects, or the way he behaves around other horses.

- Provide your horse with good care so that he is not hungry, thirsty, irritated or in pain when handled or ridden. Keep pests such as flies in control. Watch for health problems such as worms, or teeth that need to be floated, or hoof problems and take care of them promptly.

- Provide your horse with properly fitting tack. Avoid pinching straps, irritating blankets and saddle sores. Most horses know to inhale to enlarge their bellies when they are saddled. When they exhale, the saddle is loose. Put the saddle on in the barn, then walk your horse several paces and tighten the girth again before mounting.

- Choose a horse that has been properly trained and managed. Look carefully for signs of bad habits (See "Selecting the Right Horse") such as biting, kicking, rearing and bucking.

- Select a horse that has a good temperament and that is a proper match for the rider in size and training.

- Ride with someone especially if you ride trails. If you (or your horse) suffer a broken limb and are far from your home, you will have a problem getting help. You can also benefit by learning safety habits from more experienced riders.

- Be attentive. Know what is around you (vehicles, other horses or animals, people). Watch for potential dangers. Think ahead, to the next jump or water crossing and be prepared.

- Use caution when tending to a horse with an injury or illness. Even though he has never bitten or kicked before, he might if irritated or in pain. If you are changing a dressing be sure to get specific instructions from the vet or barn manager on the safest methods. For instance, if a horse has an injury on a hind leg, you can tie up one of his front legs. This way, he will not be able to kick while you are changing the dressing.

• Though most will not kick, avoid walking behind a horse, and always let the horse know where you are by approaching him without startling him.

• Small children should be watched carefully while around horses.

• If you intend to let others ride your horse, be sure that they are properly trained and aware of safety measures. Have them review and sign an agreement such as the sample "Assumption of Liability Agreement" in the appendix.

The vast majority of accidents occur due to ignorance and lack of experience. Few accidents occur while under the guidance of a professional trainer. Even the simplest command such as "shorten your left rein" from a trainer can prevent a potentially dangerous situation.

In the 20 years of the author's career, the worst accident that occurred while under her supervision was a broken arm. A child was on a pony that was completely stopped. The pony lowered his head to grab a mouthful of grass.

The child still had hold of the reins and was pulled to the ground. The arm that tried to break the fall broke itself.

By being informed, attentive and following these guidelines, you can enjoy a safe and lifelong riding career.

*Being actively involved in a lesson plan will reduce your risk of accidents.*

# JOIN THE EQUESTRIAN COMMUNITY

R iding is a sport. But unlike other sports, it involves not only athletic ability, but also the care and handling of a 1,000 pound animal. The care and handling of the horse directly effects his ability to be a safe, competitive and enjoyable mount. The rider and horse become a team. Each depends on the other. This relationship is strengthened (or weakened) by the care, training and handling of the horse by the horse owner. Take advantage of the experience of all the experts who have built the equestrian world. While searching for your horse you (and the rider if not one in the same) should:

• Purchase books or browse your library for information on horses and horse care. See the appendix for book references.

- Rent or buy videos on horse care and riding. There are excellent videos available that are advertised in equestrian journals and tack catalogs.

- Get mail order catalogs from equestrian suppliers. You can find ads for such catalogs in an equestrian magazine. These will give

*Riding is a sport that requires not only athletic ability but the care and handling of a 1,000 pound animal.*

you a good idea of the price of tack and clothing, and will have videos and books on equestrian issues. Two good mail-order houses are:

Dover Saddlery
Box 5837
Holliston, MA 01746
(800)989-1500

State Line Tack
Box 1217
Plaistow, NH 03865
(800)228-9208

• Visit forums on the on-line services and Internet sites devoted to equestrian activity. You can post specific questions, and get dozens of answers from experienced individuals anxious to help. You'll also find libraries with files on all topics, ranging from care of your horse to starting a horse business. You will find wonderful, down-to-earth, first hand testimonials on horse ownership. Most forums discourage advertising or the soliciting of business, but there are hundreds (possibly thousands) of sites on the Internet where you can get equine products and services. You will even see horses listed for sale. Just search on the keyword "horse" and you will find more than enough information.

• Put yourself in the picture - visualize yourself doing all the daily things required to manage a horse, especially if you are planning to keep your horse on your property and assume all the responsibility of care.

Riding is only one aspect of horse ownership. Picture yourself getting up before work or school *every* cold or wet morning to feed your horse and clean his stall. Or, if you board your horse, know what the expenses are going to mean to your budget. In either case, anticipate the expected and the unexpected expenses, such as an expensive injury or illness. Research and learn about mistakes instead of making them.

- Go to local shows and equestrian events. You can find them advertised in local publications or by calling the local chapter of a number of equestrian organizations such as the American Quarter Horse Association.

- Become a member of a recognized equestrian association that is geared towards your riding discipline. See the appendix for a list of associations. Many of these associations have newsletters or journals that provide specific tips on breeding, training, insurance, safety, equine medicine, preventive healthcare, tack, clothing, events and shows, etc.

- Get a subscription to a reputable horse journal such as one that is published by your equestrian association. See the Appendix for a listing of several popular publications.

- Take lessons. This will give you a good feel for the equestrian world, and help you decide what type of riding and horse you want. You should not consider purchasing a horse for someone who is not actively involved in a lesson program.

# KEEPING YOUR HORSE ON YOUR PROPERTY

Y ou must decide on whether to keep your horse on your property or board at a local barn. Either way, you should have all the plans for the care of your horse arranged before you buy your horse. You should have a boarding contract from a barn ready to sign (see the Appendix), or have your property ready with secure fencing and shelter.

If you have adequate acreage and are willing to keep your horse on your property, be prepared to devote a considerable amount of time to the care of the environment. The following is a synopsis of the issues involved:

- Riding Activities and Camaraderie

One aspect of boarding at home that you must consider is that the rider will be somewhat isolated from other riders and horses. Unless your neighbors have horses, or you intend to board other horses (then you are in the business of managing a barn), the rider may soon grow bored of the lonely atmosphere. The rider and horse will not realize the benefits of a barn where many activities take place such as show preparations, group lessons, trail rides and shared visits from the vet and farrier. You will also not have the advantage of advice and experience of the other riders and trainers.

*Show competition can boost self-esteem.*

A valuable part of owning a horse is being involved in all these activities with others who share your interests. Self esteem is boosted with healthy competition. There is also more safety when riding in pairs or groups, both from a 'buddy system' standpoint and also from learning safety tips from other more experienced riders.

*Horses are sociable herd animals and many need a pasturemate.*

Some horses also get lonely without another horse or animal. A sociable horse may be well behaved in a barn with others, but may misbehave when confined alone. He may run the fence, destroy fencing, not eat well, chew on rails, try to escape, etc. Many times a smaller grazing companion such as a goat may ease his loneliness. On the other hand, some horses are much better behaved when boarded alone.

• Local Ordinances

Many urban and suburban areas have local zoning ordinances against the housing of large animals. Check with your local county ordinances, as well as any subdivision ordinances which may apply.

Even if ordinances allow, consider your neighbors - a horse can be destructive, odorous and attract many insects and pests. He can also be an irresistible attraction for children in the area which can add to your liability.

• Acreage

You must have adequate facilities to turn out a horse and exercise him regularly. You cannot keep a horse in a garage or basement (believe it or not people have tried with disastrous results). He must have shelter, and an area large enough to walk freely. Experts disagree on the amount of acreage per horse required. This depends on how close your neighbors are, how destructive the horse is, how sturdy your fences and structures are, and how often the horse is exercised.

The results of a horse's normal everyday movements are destructive to landscaping, trees, and structures. Horses like to chew on bark,

*Fencing and structures often need repair. This gate was trampled by a thirsty horse.*

fence rails, and structures. You can keep a horse on a limited amount of property (as little as one acre) if local ordinances allow. A horse that is confined to a small paddock without the luxury of daily grazing may be more

destructive to his habitat than one that is turned out daily.
If you have a couple acres of mature, beautifully green
grass, you will still need an area to confine the horse or
your pasture will be destroyed quickly. Horse manure is
great for grass, but the grass must have time to recover
from grazing and the weight of hooves. Once your grass is
destroyed, erosion will set in, and recovery will be a long
and expensive process. Muddy, manure covered areas are
excellent breeding grounds for bacteria and parasites.

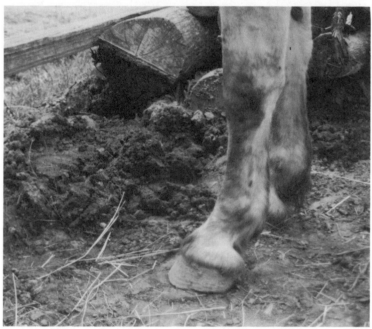

*Hooves can turn a small pasture into mud quickly.*

Structures or items in the area where the horse is kept
may be damaged. Horses can scratch, kick and bite cars,

your house, outbuildings, and farm equipment. These items can also injure the horse. If a horse is grazing near a tractor and is spooked or chased, he can easily sustain a gash that will require healing time, veterinarian expenses and possibly permanent injury. Ideally, the areas that your horse will roam will be free from obstacles and will be intended for his use alone.

Too many horses on a small piece of property can result in injuries to the horses from each other, or from stumps, holes and debris. If you keep more than one horse, you must be careful as to which horses can tolerate each other, and which ones cause trouble in a group. You may not be able to turn them all out together.

You will not only need acreage to house your horse, but also to ride on. Unless you plan to trail your horse to parks, shows or other riding facilities, riding on a small piece of property will quickly become boring and unchallenging for both horse and rider.

• Feed and Feeding

Some people mistakenly assume that you can put a horse in a pasture and the grass will be all he will need to survive. Many wild horses subsist on grass alone. But wild horses are also often in poor health, contract common preventable diseases, are not under the stress of daily riding, can starve during winter and drought, and die at earlier ages than domestic horses. Pasture grass should be considered a supplement only to a well-rounded diet. Some grasses are not suitable for grazing and can actually be harmful to your horse. Pasture should be seeded yearly with a variety of grass recommended for your climate and for horses.

The act of being turned out and allowed to roam freely are the main benefits of grazing. Grazing also keeps manure spread, improves the

*Fresh air, social interaction and the ability to freely move about are the main benefits of being turned out.*

temperament of the horse, helps prevent colic and prevents hoof ailments. You can turn horses out into areas without grass such as the riding ring, paddock or woods, but without grass to keep them occupied they may become bored and mischievous. Wooded areas are fine as long as stumps, holes and debris are managed. Pastures should have some source of shade for horses to retreat to on an extremely hot day.

Horses require hay and grain. You will need to purchase your own feed and hay, transport it from the feed store to your property and store it on your property. Hay comes in bales that are about 4'x2'x2', and grain comes in 50 or 100 pound bags. You may need a truck to transport feed and supplies from the feed store. The grain must be kept in a large, waterproof and pest proof container, or in a well-built structure with a latch that a horse cannot operate (yes, horses can learn to open some latches). If a horse can smell grain, he may break a fence or door to get to his food. Even a well fed horse will do this. If they do get into the grain, they will eat until they are extremely ill with colic which can be fatal or expensive to remedy.

Feeding and caring for a horse is a complicated subject. An act as simple as putting a horse up after exercising with a bucket of grain and plenty of water can cause severe colic and death. If you are willing to attempt to care for your horse yourself, do thorough research into the subject. Read articles, consult your veterinarian, your county extension agent and trainer, and ask the previous owner about the horse's eating habits and what he has been fed in the past. If you are an inexperienced equestrian, caring for your horse without the benefit of a professional horse trainer is not recommended and highly discouraged.

*A large hay bale for a turnout area with several horses.*

Horses eat a large amount of hay - about 1-2 pounds of hay per 100 pounds of body weight depending on amount of exercise, rate of metabolism, the quality of the hay, and the type of grain that is supplemented. A typical 1,000 pound horse can eat about 20 pounds of hay per day. Hay is only produced in the late spring and summer so you will either need to buy enough to store during the winter, or pay higher prices in the winter. Hay must be kept dry and free from mold. It is best kept off the ground in an area with good air circulation. If mold sets in, it is inedible. It also must not be used if newly cut and too green. Horses digestive tracks are delicate. Any changes in feeding, for instance, from hay to pasture grazing or from one type hay to another, must be done gradually.

For an analysis of grains and requirements based on size, activity and age and more information on equine nutrition, write:

National Academy of Science
"Nutrient Requirements of Horses"
National Academy Press
2101 Constitution Ave. NW
Washington, DC 20418-0007

• Water

You will need water facilities and buckets. Horses can drink 8 gallons of fresh water daily. You will certainly want a water source close to the water bucket. Hoses are easily destroyed by hooves and can cause injury to a horse, so they must be kept out of the paddock.

*You must insure that your horse's water does not freeze over in winter.*

During freezing temperatures, you must ensure that your horse has unfrozen water several times a day. Ponds or running water on your property may or may not provide safe drinking water and may be a hazard. Pond water should be tested periodically for contaminates.

• Disposing of waste

If your facility is large enough so that your horse can graze during the day, you will only need to clean his stall once a day. If he is confined to a paddock and fairly close (200 feet) to your nearest neighbor, you will need to clean the paddock twice a day. Horse manure is great fertilizer - but only after it has lost it's odor, and the bedding has decomposed. Until then, manure can be offensive and draw an enormous amount of flies. On a small piece of property you will have to bury it or cart it off. An effective way to bury waste is to dig a large pit, preferably with a backhoe, and use that same hole each day to dump manure into. On top of each load, pour powdered lime and some dirt to control the odor and flies. There are also organic products on the market that can speed up the decomposition of manure. This pit will have to be fenced off to avoid accidents.

Disposing of waste can be a sobering task. A single horse can produce up to 50 pounds of solid waste and 7 quarts of urine a day. This will build up quickly unless you have ample pasture to fertilize. If you are enterprising, you can compost it and give it away or sell it to neighborhood gardeners. A great arrangement would be to get a gardener or nursery to haul it away when it is fresh, leaving the composting to them.

- Bedding

The floor of your horse's stall should always have a fresh, clean layer of bedding such as wood shavings. Many types of bedding are available and each has advantages and disadvantages. You may be restricted to what is available in your area. Bedding absorbs urine and keeps the stall floor dry. This is vital for the care of hooves. Hoof problems in horses can profoundly affect their performance and can lead to disease and lameness. Without bedding, the floor of a stall will become muddy and will be difficult to clean. Bedding must be transported to your site and stored until needed. Soiled bedding and manure must be shoveled out of the stall and clean bedding shoveled into the stall each day. Many barns will truck the shavings into the aisle of the barn, and use them from the aisle as needed.

Your need for bedding will decrease if your horse is turned out often.

• Pests and insects

When you bring a horse onto your property, you will bring lots of other life along with it. Dogs, raccoons, rats, mice, opossums, and squirrels love horse grain and can eat through a plastic container. Even if your feed is tightly contained, pests will be around for the few grains that the horse misses. You will not be able to prevent all pests. Keeping them in control is the key. A proven and safe way to do this is to have a good barn cat(s) for catching mice, and perhaps a rat-catching dog such as a Jack Russell Terrier.

*A reliable mouser and a rat catching dog can be valuable in a barn.*

Flies and other insects are a major aspect of manure and horses. Again, keeping pests in control is the key. Pesticides should be used sparingly, if at all. You will not get all the insects, and you can endanger your animals, yourself and others by over applying pesticides. Some barns are even equipped with spraying systems that spray pesticides into each stall at specified time intervals. This means that the horse is not only ingesting the pesticide by breathing, but also by nibbling anything on the floor of the stall. This is not only dangerous to horses and barn visitors, but not necessary. Spider webs are great fly catchers, and there are excellent fly traps on the market that are hung

*Natural and commercial flytraps.*

away from the barn. The traps attract the flies, and soon become filled with hundreds or thousands of flies.

The most important step in controlling both pests and insects, though, is cleanliness! Prompt and proper disposal of waste well away from the barn is essential.

• Fences and Structures

Fences and structures must be built and maintained. You will need a structure for your horse to shield him from cold and wind in northern areas and the sun and heat of the

*A one horse backyard stall and hay shed.*

south. This can be a lean-to, modular or a full barn. You will need a separate structure to keep feed, hay, tools and tack. You will want to keep your feed far enough away from your horse so that he does not cause damage trying to get to it. It is not advisable to keep it near your house, because of the pests and insects it attracts.

Your barn and feed room should be accessible to a car or truck. Otherwise, you will have to carry waste, bedding, hay, grain, tack, etc. to and from the barn in a wheelbarrow. Your vet and farrier may also have a difficult time carrying their tools. Making your structures easily accessible can substantially reduce the effort involved in the everyday care of your horse. A small, 3 or 4 wheel, off-road vehicle that can pull a cart can be invaluable around a barn, and may be a necessity if the barn is not located near a road.

You may find plans for outbuildings from your local county extension agent or agricultural department. Also, read:

*Complete Plans for Building Horse Barns Big and Small* by Nancy Ambrosiano and Mary Harcourt, Breakthrough Publications, 1989.

Horses and the weather are hard on structures. Fences and structures will have to be painted and/or repaired regularly.

You will probably need to 'cross fence' your property, that is, fence it so that you have more than one confined area. This way you can separate your horses, but you can also let one area rest and reseed while the horse is grazing the other area.

There are many different types of fencing available such as wood, electric, vinyl, and barbed and each have advantages and disadvantages. Wood is fairly expensive to purchase, install and maintain but it is less harmful to horses and people. It is also more aesthetic. Electric and barbed fencing are effective and can be less expensive, but carry risks to animals and people and are unattractive. Vinyl fencing is available which never needs to be painted and is very durable, however can be expensive.

- Vets and Shoeing

You will have to schedule and deal with vet and farrier visits. The vet will visit when necessary and your horse will need shoes about once every 4-8 weeks.

- Time, time, time

You must be there *twice a day every day* to feed your horse and clean his stall, or make arrangements with a dependable individual to take on this responsibility when you are gone. That person must be willing to do all the things necessary to keep your horse healthy such as feeding, watering, turning him out and cleaning the stall. You must be there when he is sick, such as watching him for hours if he has colic. You must care for his wounds. You must find him if he gets loose, and deal with any damage that he has caused to neighboring property. Also, the more time spent in riding and caring for your horse, the better his temperament will be.

Carefully consider the time that the above activities will consume. If your horse is not fed on time, or does not have water, he could cause damage to equipment, fences, structures, or himself by trying to get to his feed and water.

- Researching the care of your horse

You should research all aspects of horse care in order to provide your horse with quality care. If you have not cared for a horse before, you should start with a barn that knows horse care rather than making potentially debilitating or fatal mistakes with your horse. Horses are not as care free as a dog or cat.

- Is it Worth it?

The obvious advantage to keeping your horse on your property is that you do not have to drive to a barn. If there is not a reputable barn near you, this may be your only option. You may be surprised if you think you will save money by keeping your horse at home. The cost of boarding vs. keeping at home can be roughly the same. You will most certainly be spending much more of your time taking care of the horse's environment than if you board your horse at a barn. Of course if you already have many acres of land and keep other farm animals, a horse may fit in very well.

Check with your local Cooperative Extension Agent. They can advise you on many of the topics listed above, and be more specific to your area and climate. Hay, pasture grasses, ponds, pests, diseases, local ordinances and climate all vary according to region and are going to impact many decisions you will be making. Your Extension Agent can provide much information that is specific to your area. This agency is usually eager to help, and their help is usually free. They may even visit your site to help with land management plans.

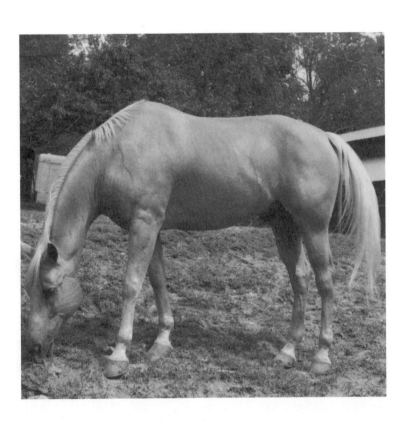

# BOARDING AT A BARN

F or the first time horse owner, boarding at a reputable barn rather than on your property is recommended. You don't have to have your horse in your backyard to enjoy riding. On the contrary, boarding at an established barn and becoming part of that supportive community can be more enjoyable.

Experienced horse handlers will take on much of your horse's care (and all of the property maintenance) so that you can spend more of your time riding, preparing for and competing in shows, and enjoying the equestrian community.

Many barns thrive in suburban and even urban areas. Your time commitment will be less if you opt to board your horse at a full service barn. However, you are still ultimately responsible for your horse's everyday health and quality of life.

You can benefit from the experience of the barn manager and other owners, and barns offer a variety of services. Some barns only offer a stall and pasture, so you must provide all the care for your horse. A barn can provide poor to excellent care for your horse. Poor care can result in health problems, poor riding performance and an unappealing riding environment. Use the questionnaire in the Appendix to evaluate barns before you sign a contract. A good barn will offer all horse care services such as:

• Feeding

The cost of boarding usually includes feed. What can be a tedious and time consuming task can be easily taken for granted by boarders. A good barn will provide dependable feeding even when you are on vacation. The barn manager can also suggest an appropriate diet for your horse. You may be charged more if your horse requires special food supplements or extra feed.

• Transportation of your horse

The barn should have a safe and dependable horse trailer as well as an experienced handler and driver. You may need transportation for trail rides, shows, breeding, veterinarian procedures that require a large animal medical facility, or moving your horse to a new location.

*The barn should offer safe transportation for your horse.*

- A reputable trainer

A reputable trainer is essential for coaching both horse and rider. A good trainer can keep your horse healthy and your riding sessions successful and safe. You will be building a relationship with your trainer and you will come to depend on your trainer for lessons and advice. Take a few lessons at the barn that you are considering. This will give you the chance to evaluate the trainer and the overall quality of the management of the barn. It cannot be over-emphasized that the rider should have taken several lessons before taking on the responsibility of owning a horse.

The horse you choose may need training to improve performance or stop a bad habit. A good horse trainer can vastly improve the riding abilities of a horse and stop potentially dangerous habits.

- Lesson plans

Most active barns will offer some lesson plans, but some offer only beginning lessons. If you are serious about your commitment to riding, you will want a wide range of

*Group activities such as shows are an important element of a full service barn.*

training. If the barn's resident trainer is limited in his or her range of instruction, the barn should offer lessons from guest trainers on a periodic basis. You should also have the option of private and group lessons, and possibly lessons restricted to adults or children.

- Shows, trail rides and other group activities

A full service barn will offer organized activities for all riders including camps for children, special clinics for adults, trail rides including transportation and involvement in shows at other locations or on site.

- Vet and Shoeing

Vet visits and farrier visits can be arranged for several horses at a time which can save money and the owners time. The barn manager can be at hand for these visits instead of the owner.

- Cleaning stalls

Daily cleaning of stalls with fresh bedding is essential for the health of your horse and to control pests and odors. Confirm that all stall floors are clean, dry and have fresh bedding.

- Caring for a sick animal

A quality barn will have an expert on hand who can spot health concerns before they become disastrous situations.

Colic and founder, hoof problems, skin diseases, and other health concerns that are not evident to inexperienced owners can be spotted in early stages by an experienced handler. The barn manager can also provide some health care maintenance such as worming, wound dressing and giving medications.

- Exercising your horse

You may not always have the time to exercise your horse. Regular riding is necessary to keep your horse in shape, just like any athlete. Regular riding and handling also benefits a horse's temperament. The more often that a horse is ridden, the better behaved and tuned he will be. If you cannot ride regularly (at least twice a week), you can either pay a qualified trainer to ride your horse, let him be used as a school horse in lessons, or have another rider at the barn ride him.

- Turn out areas

Unless a horse is ridden daily, it is important to have an area for him to run, graze, roll or just enjoy the sunshine and fresh air. Interaction with other horses is also important for many horses. A pasture with lush grass, shade trees and running water is optimum. Consider, though, the time it will take you to get your horse out of large pasture if he is turned out when you want to ride him. It will be easier to catch him if you leave a halter on, however, a halter in pasture is dangerous because it can get hung on fencing or limbs. It is better to train your horse to come to you by bringing a handful of grain or a treat each time you approach him in pasture.

*Retrieving your horse from a large pasture can be time consuming.*

Some horses are never turned out to avoid the risk of injury while in pasture. These horses, however, must be ridden daily and many horse owners feel that turning out is important to a horse's overall health and attitude.

If the turnout area has a pond, ask if it is check regularly for contaminants, and ask what the depth is. Horses can drown in 5 feet of water with a mucky bottom. You should be able to specify how your horse is turned out: only in shady areas, only with certain horses, every day, with or without halter.

- Riding areas

Adequate riding areas should be close at hand. A large riding arena, preferable with lights so that you can ride in early morning or

*A large, preferably lit riding arena is essential.*

evening is essential. An indoor arena is great in areas with substantial rainfall. Riding trails on the property, or easy access to riding trails is important for those who like trails.

- Adequate stalls

Stalls should be at least 10 feet by 10 feet, and 10 feet high. Bedding should be fresh and clean. Good cross ventilation throughout the barn is very important. Horses should not share stalls and they should be in assigned stalls.

*Look for roomy, clean stalls with good ventilation.*

- Tack room

You will want to keep your tack at the barn to avoid hauling it back and forth. You should have access to a neat, room, ventilated tack room that is close to the barn. All rider's tack should be respected.

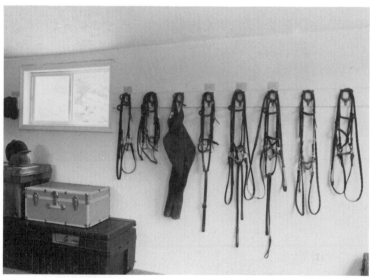

*You should have access to a clean, roomy tack room.*

- Buying and selling activity

Some barn managers will agree to assist in the sale of a horse by advertising, finding potential buyers, and showing the horse to buyers.

- The Barn Manager/Trainer

The barn manager is important in several ways. Not only will you rely on him/her for instruction, advice and the excellent care of your horse, but also to provide a well rounded riding environment for all boarders. Even the most expensive barns can employ managers who are difficult to deal with and truly don't care about the well being of your horse or your riding career. A barn manager should freely give you honest advice, and not keep important information to himself, which makes him look like the "expert".

The barn manager's first concern should be your safety and that of your horse. All activities should be supervised. A barn manager should be firm and observant. And, of course, you should feel that you can develop a trusting and comfortable relationship with the barn manager.

- Costs of boarding

Monthly costs for boarding can vary depending on all the services and factors mentioned above. Your monthly fee will range from $125 to $500. Remember that when you compare barn prices to compare the complete package. The extra $100 per month that you may pay at a well managed barn which offers extensive group activities and lessons may be well worth it. You may be able to get a discount on the board if you allow the trainer to use your horse as a school horse. You also may negotiate for a lower fee if you are willing to clean stalls or feed horses, but you will probably find that the reduction in fee is not worth your time and labor, although this can be a good lesson in responsibility and earning for a child. You probably will not be allowed to feed only your horse yourself, because once all the horses know the grain is coming, they are impatient to get theirs. All the horses must be fed in quick succession or some can damage stalls or injure themselves.

Many barns will not let owners negotiate to muck only their own horse's stalls because they find that some owners do not follow through on the promise. Any good barn owner cannot bear to see a horse, even though it is not his own, live in poor conditions. The barn manager is then left with the task.

Boarding costs may drop as you go further away from a large city. Land, feed, labor, cost of transportation are all cheaper farther away from a large city. Do not go so far out that you will be unwilling to visit your horse often. It should be close enough so that you can ride after work or school during the week.

Take your time in choosing a barn. The barn should be neat, tack room neat, and the tack of owners respected. Feed should be free of pests. Hay should not be damp or have a musty odor. Use the checklist in the Appendix. Make several copies and fill it out for each barn you visit. If you visit several, you may forget important details on each barn unless you record them. While you are looking at barns, you will also be able to see a good variety of horses and you can start comparing their traits. You will also meet many people who can put you in touch with horses for sale.

You can find barns listed in the yellow pages under Stables or Riding Academies. Suburban areas that are close to rural areas will have the largest concentration of horse facilities. Find a few, call them and arrange a visit.

Choose a barn whose primary concern is your horse's well being. Don't be influenced by expensive surroundings that don't add to the quality of care of the horses. Try not to choose your barn based solely on location. And choose your barn or prepare your facility *before* you choose your horse. Avoid the situation where you have chosen a horse and then must make a hasty decision on his boarding arrangements.

# EXPENSES

n addition to boarding, there are other expenses that you should be aware of prior to buying your horse. Here is a description of the expenses you will encounter. There is a summary of expenses at the end of the chapter.

## VETERINARY CARE

- General Care

Your horse will need to be checked by a vet before purchase. Throughout the life of your horse, you will need worming treatments, dental care ("floating" the teeth), treatment for injuries or illnesses and vaccinations, and shoeing. Your healthcare bills will vary widely depending on your location, your healthcare professional's fees, and the injuries or illnesses your horse develops. You can reduce the cost of vet visits if you schedule them with other boarders at the same barn. And, as is true with all healthcare, preventive measures are always less costly and more effective than treating a preventable injury or illness.

- Worming

While grazing, horses ingest the larvae and eggs of worms that are passed in the manure of an infected animal. The most dangerous worms, strongyle, hatch in the intestinal track and burrow through to blood vessels where they suck blood for several weeks. Then they enter the intestine again, lay eggs, and continue the cycle. Worms can cause colic, poor performance, poor coats, itching, shorter life span and an increased need for grain in your horse.

Although you can buy worming remedies yourself, your vet can recommend a worming program that is right for your area and horse. Worming may be needed as little as twice a year or as much as every four weeks depending on the concentration of horses in the same grazing area.

- Immunizations

Horses are susceptible to several diseases. Tetanus is the most prevalent. The farm environment is conducive to harboring Tetanus and horses are particularly susceptible to the disease. Other immunizations are available that prevent Encephalomyelitis, Equine Influenza, Leptospirosis, Stangles, Rhinopneumonitis, and rabies. Your veterinarian can advise the best immunization program for your horse. Keep records of your horse's immunizations.

Another disease, which does not have an immunization, is equine infectious anemia, or EIA. EIA can be debilitating or life threatening, or a horse can carry the disease without showing any symptoms for life. The carrier can also infect other horses. EIA is spread by blood either by biting flies or using syringes on more than one horse. The disease has been controlled by testing all horses, destroying or quarantining carriers, and the use of disposable syringes. In the United States, a current negative "Coggin's test" is required for any horse being bought or sold, raced, shown or crossing state lines. This is an essential test to look for when reviewing the health records of a horse that you may buy.

Your horse may need special dietary supplements or vitamins which your vet can recommend.

Preventive care is the key to health for your horse, and to lower vet bills. Prevention always costs less than treatment. If you let conditions such as worms or poor dental care get out of control, your horse will suffer and you will eventually suffer huge vet bills, a misbehaving and ill-performing horse and heartache.

## DENTAL CARE

Unlike human teeth, horses teeth continue to grow during their lifetime because horses are grazing animals. Horses teeth must be regularly "floated". The molars must be actually filed down so that the horse can grind his grain. If they are not filed down, mouth ulcers can occur. The horse then has difficulty grinding his grain and getting the proper nutrition. Most horses will need their teeth floated every 9-18 months. Most vets provide this service, but some farriers also are trained in equine dental care.

## SHOEING

Most horses require shoes on two or four feet even if they are ridden on the best surfaces. Horses also routinely need their hooves trimmed. A professional who shoes horses is correctly referred to as a "farrier" (not a "blacksmith", who is a person who works with ornamental iron).

Shoeing should not be taken for granted. Incorrect shoeing can amplify a bad trait and can even contribute to an injury. On the other hand, a good farrier can actually improve a horse's "way-of-going" and soundness.

Shoes will be fitted differently depending on the type of riding your intend to do. Usually a farrier specializes in a certain type. If you have chosen a reputable barn, the barn manager will have a reputable farrier. The cost of shoeing varies depending on number of shoes, whether special corrective shoes are necessary, whether you can share the cost of the visit with other boarders, how often the horse wears them out and the condition of the horses feet.

## TACK

Riding horses is a sport much like all other sports. You need a coach, lessons, the right gear and the right clothes. "Gear" is called "tack" in the horse world. You can easily spend between $500 and $10,000 on tack for your horse. If

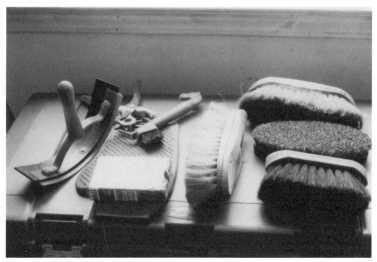

*Grooming accessories.*

you plan to show, plan to spend more. Your tack will also have to be regularly cleaned and cared for. There is much more to tack than saddle and bridle. You will also need saddle blankets, a crop, halter, girth guard, hoof pick, lead rope, and brushes. Your horse may need a turn-out blanket, martingale, or other specialized equipment.

Many riders maintain separate tack for showing. They have one bridle for everyday riding, and one more expensive bridle for showing.

The performance of some horses is improved with specialized tack such as a martingale. However, often these horses require the specialized equipment because they have not been trained properly or have bad habits. A horse that must be forced into a frame with restricting tack rather than trained into the frame is not for a beginner.

When purchasing tack, keep in mind that cheap items may cause you or your horse pain, and will not retain much resale value. You can buy a $200 saddle, but it probably will not be orthopedically correct for your horse or you. Your horse will not move as well, your legs may be pinched and it will lose its value quickly. On the other hand, a used $1000 saddle with proper care will keep much of its resale value. If you can't afford new, look for used, high quality tack. Good quality tack that is properly maintained can last years.

Used tack should be thoroughly cleaned to prevent the spread of skin or respiratory diseases. Just as when buying new tack, be sure that it fits your horse and you properly. Do not assume that if your horse comes with tack, it is properly fitting or proper for your type of riding. Use the advice of your trainer to select proper, good fitting tack. You can find ads for used tack in barns or local publications.

Tack varies depending on your riding discipline. The major two types of tack are Western and English. English can be hunt seat, dressage, saddle seat or combined training. Western can be stock, roping, reining, or pleasure. Each type also has various sizes for children and adults. Bridles, bits and saddles vary depending on these classifications. Western saddles are the classic cowboy saddle, with a horn and pommel to rest your hands on, large stirrups and are often ornamentally carved or decorated. English saddles are lighter, smaller and more plain. They do not have a horn, and have simple steel stirrups. If the rider is a child, break-away stirrups are recommended for English and a toe guard for Western. With these stirrups, the riders foot will not get stuck in the stirrup if thrown. Other stirrups can allow the foot to go completely through and if the rider is thrown he will be dragged and trampled.

Bridles also differ depending on the type of riding you plan, and the needs of the horse. Again, your trainer can help you decide.

And of course, with all this expensive equipment you will need a large, secure tack trunk or closet.

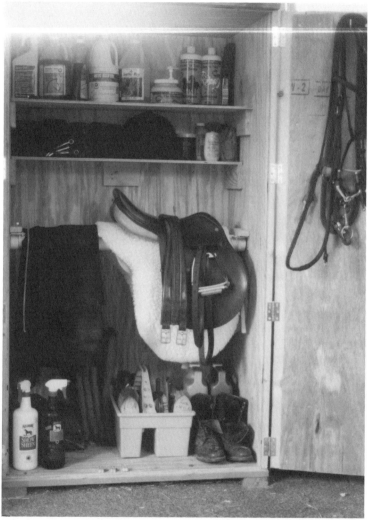

*A well equipped and neat tack closet.*

You can buy tack in local tack stores or by mail-order. A trip to the tack store, with the smell of leather, the ability to touch the products, try on clothes, and interact with other horse lovers is always fun. Mail order will give you a larger selection. Call for a free catalog to compare prices:

Dover Saddlery
Box 5837
Holliston, MA 01746
(800)989-1500

State Line Tack
Box 1217
Plaistow, NH 03865
(800)228-9208
Specify English or Western.

For a detailed discussion of all types of tack, see

*Tack Buyer's Guide*, by Charlene Strickland, Breakthrough Publications, Inc., 1988.

## LESSONS

It is surprising how many people want to buy a horse before they have even taken their first lesson. The importance of lessons cannot be overemphasized and is often overlooked by the first time horse buyer. As mentioned earlier, riding horses is a sport just like golf, soccer, tennis, etc. Every team or player has a coach and is constantly improving the game with instructional practice. This is not only important to enjoy the sport, but vitally important to maintaining safety. We strongly recommend 2 years of lessons from a reputable instructor before purchasing your first horse. This will give you the opportunity to ride several different types of horses and develop preferences so that when you are ready to buy, you will know what you want.

During lessons, an experienced trainer can spot problems before they develop into dangerous situations. Here are a few examples:

• The owner has chosen tack that does not fit the horse properly, or the tack is not put on properly. This results in pain and/or irritation to the horse which results in (best case) poor performance by the horse or (worst case) biting, kicking, and bucking. The horse will also tend to misbehave during tacking up because he knows he is in for an unpleasant experience.

• The horse begins to refuse at jumps. This results in (best case) poor performance and frustration for horse and rider, or (worst case) throwing the rider. This obviously can be extremely dangerous. A trainer can spot riding faults that contribute to refusals and coach the rider in how to keep this bad habit from forming.

• The horse bolts through gates as soon as they are open. Many gates are positioned so that they swing closed rather than stay open. An inexperienced handler often does not open the gate enough or prevent the gate from swinging shut on the horse's rump. The gate can also catch the hips and cause and injury. Pretty soon, the horse learns to bolt through the gate to avoid the startling slap of the gate. An alert trainer can spot poor handling of a horse and teach the student how to avoid these situations.

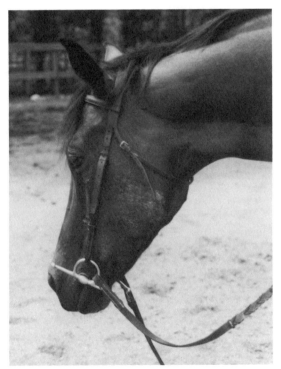

*Bit too loose; throat-strap too tight. An instructor can correct ill-fitting tack to avoid bad behavior or poor performance.*

There are many subtle aspects to riding, training and caring for a horse that when brought together produce a successful riding pair. An ongoing lesson program is essential to this success.

## CLOTHING

Proper riding gear is more than just fashion. Just as poorly fitting or substandard tack can irritate a horse, poor

*At the very least, every rider needs proper boots and protective headgear.*

quality clothing can hinder the rider from enjoying the sport and excelling. At the least, the rider needs excellent shoes or boots and headgear that is approved by the American Horse Show Association.

Clothes should be specifically designed for riding. Improper shoes can slip from the stirrup. Tennis shoes around the barn will not protect your toes if a horse steps on your foot. Better clothing will make riding more comfortable and safe.

Correct clothing is important in the show ring. Attending a couple horse shows in your area for your type of riding will give you a good indication of what is appropriate. Pay attention to what the winners are wearing. Refer to a journal related to your riding discipline for details on show clothing trends.

Clothing can be obtained through retail tack stores in suburban/rural areas, or through various mail order catalogues. See the section above on "Tack" for mail-order catalogs. Tack catalogs include riding clothes and accessories.

## INSURANCE

Owning a horse brings inherent risks that you will want coverage for. You can obtain liability insurance in case your horse causes injury, surgical insurance for that unexpected accident or ailment, and mortality insurance that pays at the time of death of the horse.

Your risk of a lawsuit increases when you let other people ride your horse. Be ready to make firm rules about who rides your horse. See the sample Assumption of Liability Agreement in the Appendix.

Of course, cost and types of coverage will vary widely from state to state. Start with your homeowner's insurance company and see if they provide it or can refer to a company which specializes in such risk. You can find insurers who specialize in equestrian policies through advertisements in local equestrian publications. You can also obtain insurance through the American Horse Show Association by becoming a member.

————————————————

Horses vary widely in breeding, health, age, ability and size. These factors determine cost. Know what your budget is before you start your search. The price of a horse can be between $0 and $50,000, but note that the purchase price of the horse is minor in comparison to the amount of money you will spend on his care. A free horse can cost as much to board as the $20,000 horse. And chances are, the "free" horse is appropriately priced because he probably has a serious handling problem, health concern or is just not suited for riding. That free horse may end up costing the unsuspecting buyer hundreds or thousands in training, vet bills and boarding and then may not even be ridable. Don't let the costs of boarding, feed, vet bills, tack, lessons and clothing take you by surprise. Following is a chart summarizing the expenses of horse care. If you hope to own a horse on a particularly tight budget, read Sharon Smith's *The Affordable Horse* (1994, Howell Book House).

The table on the following page summarizes the expenses that you can expect while owning a horse.

## SUMMARY OF EXPENSES

| Expenses | Cost Range per Year | Comments |
|---|---|---|
| **Boarding** | $1,500-6,000 | Depends on location and facilities. Costs to board on your property will be comparable. |
| **Veterinarian** | $90-2,000 | Depends on number and severity of injuries or illnesses |
| **Tack** | $500-10,000 | More tack is required for showing |
| **Lessons once a week** | $1,200-2,400 | Necessary! |
| **Clothing** | $150 - 5,000 | Higher if showing |
| **Shoeing** | $80 - 400 | Depends on number of shoes and quality of the horse's feet |
| **Total Yearly Costs** | **$3,520 - 25,800** | |

# LEASING A HORSE

easing a horse prior to purchasing is a great way to get a good sense of horse ownership. Beginning riders often do not realize how challenging horse ownership can be. Leasing can give a rider a realistic yet temporary glance at horse ownership.

Many barns will lease a horse which will give you a fairly realistic idea of the commitment you are about to make. This will cost less than owning and caring for the horse. The cost depends on the length of the lease and whether you are willing to let others ride the horse during your lease. The horse may be a school horse which will be unavailable to you while another rides him for a lesson. The cost and arrangements of a lease are flexible and can be negotiated with the horse and barn owner. By the time your lease is up, you will know if this is the horse for you (if he is for sale) or at least you will have a good idea of the qualities that you are looking for in a horse.

## LEASING A HORSE

You can lease a very expensive horse for a season rather than owning him. For instance, for $2,000 you might lease a $10,000 show quality hunter/jumper. You may find leases at more reasonable rates during the off season - late Fall through early Spring. An exceptional horse that is only ridden by a student during the summer may be available for lease in the Fall and Winter.

If the rider is a student, you may find that a summer lease is the only practical solution. But if this is the case, you may want to reconsider full time horse ownership.

If you find a suitable horse and come to a verbal understanding of a lease with the owner, be sure you get all the details in writing. Have a lease contract that you understand ready to sign. The contract should cover:

- the lease length

- terms of payment

- is this an exclusive lease, or can others ride the horse during the lease (including the owner(s))?

- type of insurance that is required and who pays

- liability issues (who pays for medical, personal or property damages incurred during the lease period)

- boarding fees (will you, or the owner be responsible for boarding during the lease?)

- use of any tack

- whether or not the leasee can transport the horse to events and trails

- how the horse will be ridden

- farrier and vet expenses during the lease

- any other specifics related to your agreement with the owner

For more information, see the Sample Lease Contract in the Appendix.

---

The aim of the previous chapters is to mentally prepare you for the large responsibility and expenses that you are about to undertake. Be realistic and truthful with yourself. By now, you should know that riding the horse is only one aspect of owning a horse. The total package consists of many other equally important (and rewarding) tasks.

Hopefully, after reading these chapters you are more committed than ever to owning a horse. You are ready to accept horse ownership with both eyes open to all the issues. The real horse lover will be anxious to take on all the challenges and expenses described above. If you're still in, congratulations, and read on!

# Section Two: Finding and Purchasing Your Horse

# FINDING GOOD HORSES FOR SALE

orses are priced based on a variety of factors. In order for you to judge the value of any horse, you must compare to many others that are close in quality. Here are some sources to find good horses for sale:

## NEWSPAPERS

City newspapers will have a classified section for horses and horse equipment. If you live in a remote area of your state, you may actually have to drive closer to a suburban area to find equestrian activity and a good selection of horses. Most equestrian activity is between urban and rural areas, where the population is high enough to support such activities, and land is reasonably priced. Check these area newspapers for classified ads.

## YOUR STATE'S AGRICULTURAL BULLETIN

One of the best sources of advertisements is the agricultural bulletin published by your state government. A subscription to this bulletin is often free and can be obtained by calling the State government department of Agriculture.

The contact for the state of Georgia is:
Department of Agriculture
19 Martin Luther King Jr. Drive
Atlanta, GA 30334-4250
(404)656-3722

One downside to this, however, is that many of the horses may be throughout the state and not convenient to your area. The State's agricultural bulletin is valuable for other reasons, though. You can use it to compare prices of horses, tack, feed, equipment, trailers and farm acreage.

## TACK AND FEED STORES

Local tack stores or feed stores often have bulletin boards that advertise horses for sale. You can also get good information from store owners on reputable nearby barns and horse brokers.

## LOCAL PUBLICATIONS OF SPECIALTY ADVERTISING

If your suburban or rural area has many equestrian facilities and events, you will probably find a publication devoted to horse interests. Tack and feed stores usually carry these publications. Your area may even have a publication devoted to horse trading. Here are a few good examples:

The Horsetrader (national publication)
P.O. Box 728
8398 Bundysburg Rd
Middlefield, OH  44062
(800)837-0066

Farm and Dairy (agricultural weekly in Ohio with an equine page each month)
185-205 East State Street
Salem, Ohio  44460
(800)837-3419

Horseman's News  (California all-breed advertiser)
P.O. Box 2229
San Marcos, CA  92079
(800)817-7259

Ride!  (California, Western Nevada and So Oregon)

728 Cherry Street
Chico, CA 95928
(916)343-9994
Email: smorton@wsmith.com
http://www.ridemag.com

The Paper Horse (Mainly Pennsylvania)
R.R. #4
Box 405
Mifflintown, PA 17059
(717)436-8893

StableMates (entire Southeast)
P.O. Box 89
Royston, GA 30662
(800)782-6283
http://stablemates.com

## RACETRACKS

Most retired racing horses are registered Thoroughbreds under 6 years old, and many are perfectly suitable for pleasure riding and showing for many years. At age 6 a horse is just entering his prime riding years. Thousands of horses are retired from racetracks yearly because they could be lame, or simply not fast enough for the race tack, but can make exceptional hunter/jumpers and pleasure horses. In fact, one of the horses on the 1996 U.S. Olympic Equestrian Team was acquired for $600 from a race track. Most require additional training for a beginning rider, but some are quite suitable for an intermediate or advanced rider. A horse from the track will have a number tattooed inside his upper lip, indicating his birthyear and the last 4 numbers of his registration certificate.

Trainers would much rather place these horses in homes than send them to slaughter. To solicit a castoff, and advertise to trainers who would have castoffs, contact:

*"Buddy" is retired from the track.*

Horsemen's Benevolent and Protective Association
2800 Grand Route
Saint John Street
New Orleans, LA  70119
(504) 945-4500

This is the national headquarters.  They should be able to give you the number of a branch that is associated with a local thoroughbred track.  Contact the track and ask if they have a similar organization or if they can put you in touch with a trainer  who can locate castoffs  for potential homes.

Another organization that is active in placing castoffs is:

California Equine Retirement Foundation
34033 Kooden Road
Winchester, CA  95366
714-925-4190

Remember that these organizations exist on donations, and provide a great service to the equestrian community, so be sure to contribute if they help you find a horse.

## BARNS

Visit local barns.  If the barn has a sign offering lessons or horses for sale, they will welcome visitors.  Use your visits not only to hunt for available horses, but also to evaluate the barn as a potential boarding and training facility. This will also give you an opportunity to compare several horses at the same time. Look for barns that specialize in the type of riding that interests you.

## BREEDERS

You may be lucky enough to live near a breeder who specializes in your favorite breed. If you are set on a specific breed, you should subscribe to an equestrian journal that specializes in your type of riding. These journals will have ads from the major breeding farms. Most of their offerings, however, will be untrained foals or breeding mares. You will have to invest considerable time and money into training if you opt for a foal. You are also gambling on the horse's unproved temperament. This option is for the more experienced rider.

## ON-LINE SERVICES

Forums in on-line computer services and sites on the Internet include areas to post "for sale" horses, but since the on-line services are used by people all over the world, your chances of finding a horse near you is slim. However, the information is valuable for comparison purposes. You can also post a "Horse Wanted" notice for free.

## YOUR INSTRUCTOR OR TRAINER

The rider should have had several lessons before considering horse ownership. Assuming so, your instructor will be an excellent source of information or may agree to act as a broker or consultant in finding a horse. A good instructor has a network of people and establishments in the equestrian world and can usually locate a suitable horse. Your trainer also has the best knowledge of the rider's skill level and can choose a good match. Expect to pay a fee for this service. See "Involving an Expert" under "Evaluating the Horse" later for more information.

## LOCAL EQUESTRIAN SHOWS AND EVENTS

Local shows and events may have postings of horses for sale. Events are usually advertised in local horse publications, tack stores, barns and through equestrian associations such as the Pony Club or American Quarter Horse Association.

## EQUESTRIAN ASSOCIATIONS

As a horse owner, you should be a member of an equestrian association. You can find the names of associations in a magazine dealing with your type of riding, or in the Appendix. Associations provide many benefits including communication, events, referrals on instructors and trainers, discounts on products and even insurance. Horses for sale are sometimes advertised through these associations.

## AUCTIONS

You may find auctions in rural areas or in areas known for horse breeding. For the inexperienced buyer, auctions are risky. You will not have the opportunity to test-drive the animal or sufficient time to determine his temperament. You will have to make an instant decision. Auctions are mainly for experienced horse traders who can spot potential in an untrained young horse. If you are working with a broker or trainer, they can help you at an auction.

---

Buy from a reputable dealer or an honest independent owner. Your chances of paying a fair price and getting a sound horse (or at least truthful information about his soundness) are much greater with a dealer whose business and reputation mean more than a one time sale. A good dealer is not going to endanger his reputation by misleading a buyer or trying to sell a horse that is unsound or unsafe. Ask about the dealer at local tack stores or barns.

# SELECTING A GREAT HORSE

H ow much you spend on your horse will depend on your budget. Consider that soon you will spend many thousands of dollars per year in caring for your horse. This includes boarding (or property maintenance), tack, riding clothes, vet bills, shoeing, training and lessons. It can cost just as much to care for a $500 animal as it does to care for the $15,000 animal. Sometimes, the $500 horse will end up costing even more in vet bills or training because he is priced lower due to health, inadequate training or inability to perform.

Take your time and be willing to invest enough money on the purchase price of the horse to get the best animal and the best fit for the rider. The perfect horse will have sound temperament and will be matched to the rider's size and ability.

## Considering the "Free" Horse, a Wild Horse or an Abused or Neglected Horse

- The "Free" Horse

You may be in a situation where a friend wants to give you a horse because you happen to own a few acres and he has a horse that he cannot properly care for. He may be giving you a $400 animal, but you will soon spend thousands of dollars in caring for him and preparing the environment. The experience may be a heartache and may ruin a young rider's aspirations.

The rider will be much more successful if the horse is hand picked and matched to his/her abilities. This section deals with *selecting* your horse - you should be discriminating while searching for your horse.

Consider also that the "free" horse is free for a reason. No one is going to give away a sound, good tempered animal. The horse may have a dangerous habit or may be unhealthy.

- The Abused or Neglected Horse

You may come across an obviously neglected or abused horse that is free or relatively inexpensive. It will be heartbreaking and tempting to consider taking one in.

Though these horses truly need and deserve a good home and tender loving care, they are not for the beginning owner. Most will be hard to handle and will have health concerns. Caring for one takes enormous patience and experience.

Instead of adopting an animal in poor condition, consider calling one of the rescue services listed below. Some communities have chapters devoted to equine issues. These organizations are well equipped to find appropriate homes for the horses. They can also pursue any legal charges that might apply against the owner. Follow up and make sure that the animal was taken care of.

Colorado Horse Rescue
Box 1510
Arvada, CO   80001-1510
(303)469- 5863

American Horse Protection Assoc.
1000 29th Street NW
Ste T-100
Washington, DC  20007
(202)965-0500

American Society for the Prevention of Cruelty to Animals (ASPCA)
424 East 92nd street
New York, NY  10128

(212)876-7700

Hoofed Animal Humane Society
Box 400
Woodstock, Il 60098
(815)337-5563

Humane Society of the United States
2100 1 Street NW
Washington, DC 20037
(202)452-1100

These organizations rely on donations to provide this protective service to horses.

- A Wild Horse

The Bureau of Land Management organizes the adoption of wild horses from the Western plains.

Wild horses are perhaps the most challenging to train and to acclimate to domestic conditions. Wild horses from the American West are small, usually under 15 hands high (60 inches). The fee for adoption is $125, ($75 for a wild burro) and you must pay for transportation. You will also end up paying a great deal of money to train a wild horse, that may or may not turn out to be suitable for riding. This option is not recommended for a beginning or intermediate rider. For more information, write:

Adopt-a-horse
Bureau of Land Management
US Dept. of the Interior
Washington, DC 20240
(202)653-9215

Bureau of Land Management
Jackson District Office
411 Briarwood Drive
Suite 404
Jackson, MS  39206

Wild horses are sometimes transported to Eastern states and auctioned there. For more information call your State Department of Agriculture.

Also, for more information on all the issues involved in dealing with a wild horse:

*The Wild Horse: An Adopter's Manual*, by Barbara Eustis-Cross and Nancy Bowkers, Howell Book House 1992.

For an excellent discussion on selecting free or low-cost riding horses, read:

*The Affordable Horse*, by Sharon B. Smith, Howell Book House, 1994.

Typical riding horses, for pleasure and local show competition can range from $500 to $15,000. Factors to consider when selecting your horse are:

## TEMPERAMENT

Good temperament, or disposition, should be your first concern when selecting a horse. Think of your horse as an athlete. He can be great looking, muscular, and talented but he must be willing and cooperative to develop these qualities to become a great athlete. A horse with an even temperament will not only be safer, he will also respond to the rider more readily and learn faster.

Temperament is the horse's behavior, his disposition, or his ability to be handled willingly and without danger. A good tempered horse:

- is consistent and predictable,
- allows a variety of people (men, women and children) to approach and handle him,
- tolerates other horses nearby,
- stands still while grooming, girthing, vetting, loading and shoeing,
- behaves in a show or on a trail as if he was in his ring at home (calm, responsive and deliberate in his movements),

- does not pin his ears when approached or when handled,
- does not spook at sudden sounds or images such as a flag or sign,
- does not bite, kick, rear or buck,
- most importantly, reflects a horse with heart who wants to please.

Great temperament can definitely increase the value of a horse. This may be somewhat difficult to judge unless you spend an adequate amount of time with the horse, riding and providing care.

Beginning riders often loose their balance which can result in inadvertently yanking on the reins or plopping on the horses back. This will hurt or irritate the horse. Some horses can tolerate this and some cannot. If you are choosing a horse for a beginning rider, be sure to choose one that can tolerate the mistakes of a beginner. This is the horse that is well trained, and has a good temperament. Some horses are completely tolerant and even seem to "take care" of their inexperienced riders. Others size up their rider immediately and take advantage of the situation.

Usually, the horse that has been well trained, ridden consistently by a fairly good rider, is healthy, and has been well cared for will have an even temperament. Temperament is greatly influenced by the methods of handling the horse. Subtle mishandling of a horse can encourage bad temperament and bad habits. Usually there is a specific reason that a horse "misbehaves". He is irritated, in pain, hungry, thirsty, or associates these sensations with an event or activity. For instance, you can load a horse into a trailer calmly, using many tricks to gently coax him on. If he has been loaded before by using a whip, or if he has been in a trailer accident, he logically will not like the loading process and will be frightened and dangerous when he is loaded. However, horses like humans, have distinct and individual personalities and cannot always be molded into our ideals. Some will simply have bad dispositions no matter how well they are cared for. And of course, some are sweet and gentle from the beginning. A horse can also change during his lifetime as he matures, either mellowing out or becoming more cranky.

The horse with a great temperament will not change hands often. Either the owners hold on to him because of his even temper, or his temper is even due to years of consistent loving care. Beware of the horse that has changed hands many times. Your best way to determine disposition is to spend enough time with the horse to confirm the present owner's claims of good temperament. Chances are there is a reason that he was not suitable as a long-term riding partner. Ask previous owners, other barn boarders, his vet and others questions about his disposition and other traits. If your horse has registration papers, you will see the list of owners. If not, you may have difficulty in finding previous owners. You may not get completely honest answers, but you should consider inconsistencies in answers as a red flag. The best find would be the horse that has had consistent, quality care from a single owner.

The trait of being "spirited" or "high strung" can be a reflection of poor temperament, or inadequate training. A horse needs discipline and years of training and consistent quality riding to behave as a successful mount. Many people think that a spirited horse is valued. On the contrary, most show horses and successful riding horses are quiet but responsive. The overly spirited horse may look beautiful running in a pasture, but may be unpredictable, and difficult to handle and ride. This type of horse is not suitable for a beginning rider, but can make a challenging partner for an experienced rider.

Good temperament should not be confused with lethargy. A good tempered horse will be quiet and cooperative, but will also be responsive and alert. You will find horses that are quite, docile and fairly easy to handle, but they may also be unresponsive to the riders commands and sluggish in the ring. This may be a great school horse for the beginning rider, but will eventually be frustrating and will not benefit a rider who is trying to progress and learn.

There is little association between age and temperament. A 4 year old horse that has been properly trained, cared for and consistently ridden can be just as quiet and manageable as a 10 year old. Also, a 10 year old can still be quite spirited with a mean disposition.

Some breeds display certain temperaments. Though there are exceptions, thoroughbreds and Arabians are high-strung, while Quarter horses and grade horses are more quiet. Like dogs, pedigreed horses sometimes have conformation faults, bad attitudes, and are not as tough as the mixed breeds. A grade horse (mixed breed) is perfectly acceptable as a beginning show horse, and often escapes some of these inbred faults.

Horses, like people, have personalities. Talk to any horse owner and they will tell you, in great detail, about their horse's personality. You will be amazed at the differences in personalities. Horses can be eager or unwilling, gentle or rough, competitive or non-competitive, playful or loaners, passive or aggressive, etc. All of these qualities can add to or detract from the purchase price and affect their ability to be trained and to be good riding partners.

## BREEDS

Bloodlines of the horse can have a huge impact on cost. A completely untrained and unproved horse with exceptional ancestry will command a high price. Add professional training, proven show experience and temperament, and this will be the most expensive horse.

A breed horse with papers is not always necessary for successful riding and showing in most show associations. A grade horse (mixed breed) is often a better choice for the beginning rider, and often an excellent choice for an experienced rider. The only exception to this is when the rider intends to compete in shows requiring specific breeds. Most show associations and riding disciplines do not require a specific breed, or offer "open class" categories for competition.

Note that there are no regulations on the amount of "line" breeding that can occur in a pedigree. Though opinions vary among breeders and trainers it is the opinion of the authors that line breeding is not desirable. Look closely at the horse's pedigree to see if the same name(s) appear several times in the line. This indicates inbreeding.

A horse's papers can be valuable information. Past owners are listed. You can call them for information on the horse's personality, why they sold him, his show record, bad habits, and possibly past sales prices.

Many highly specialized breeds of horses have been developed throughout the years. Since you are seriously considering horse ownership, you probably have studied books that illustrate the different breeds. Most of these books picture a champion from each breed as an example. Though these are lovely pictures, these horses are hardly representative of the typical riding and pleasure horse.

Purebred horses do not necessarily perform better or make better riding partners. On the contrary, as stated above, some breeds tend to be high strung, or have faults due to inbreeding. Some of the most successful show competitors, including Olympic competitors are "grade" horses, that is, mixed breed horses. Also, not every horse in a certain breed will be a good performer. Some will be poor while others will be exceptional, and this will be reflected in the price.

If you are considering a certain breed, contact an association for the breed and study the characteristics and breeding guidelines. These associations will welcome your questions. The breeds that have the most horses will have stronger associations, more of a population to choose from (with less inbreeding), more organized shows, activities, breeders and journals. Some of the larger breed associations are listed in the appendix.

## AVOIDING THE HORSE WITH BAD HABITS

Though their main method of defense is flight, ANY horse can bite and/or kick under certain circumstances. Handling problems can cause injury to horse, handler, equipment and structures. Your liability risk increases greatly with a horse that has bad habits. Some are tough to spot but well worth the effort to avoid. Your best chance of spotting these traits is to spend as much time as possible with him, handling and riding him. You can also talk to many people who know the horse: veterinarian, farrier, owner, barn manager, previous owners, other boarders, other riders. You may not get truthful answers from all, but your should investigate inconsistencies in answers.

With professional training, some of the bad habits listed below can be reversed. However, a horse with one of these habits is not recommended for the beginning rider.

- Biting and Kicking

Horses usually bite or kick for a reason. They are irritated, hungry, thirsty, in pain or competing with other horses. Times when a horse is apt to bite and kick are during feeding, while girthing or mounting, while a mare is in estrous, when the horse has an injury, or when irritants such as flies are not under control.

Some horses are apt to bite and kick more than others. A gelding near a mare in season, and certainly a stallion near a mare in season may bite. A mare is also more likely to bite during estrous than when not in season.

Biting and kicking is not only a threat to people it is also a threat to stablemates. Horses can be aggressive towards

*Ear Pinning Prior to Biting*

each other while riding in a group or at pasture. An overly aggressive horse may have to be turned out in isolation which will probably increase your boarding fees. You may also be liable for damages to the other horses that your horse inflicts.

One sign that indicates that a horse is ready to bite is "ear pinning". The horse flattens his ears. If you see this while watching the horse, this is a good indication that he has a bad attitude and is not for a beginning rider.

**114**

Another clue to look for is whether the horse has bitten the rails or kicked at planks on the inside of his stall. Of course the damage could have been done by the previous occupant of the stall, and not all horses that chew or kick rails are apt to so the same to people or other horses. Chewing and kicking inanimate objects is a habit to avoid, though. You will be responsible for any damage caused by your horse at the boarding facility, just as you would if boarding on your property.

The seller may indicate truthfully that the horse has not been known to kick or bite, but he cannot guarantee that the horse will not in the future. A quiet horse that has been lovingly cared for who is sold to a negligent owner can develop a temperament that is conducive to kicking and biting. And, even if lovingly cared for, any horse can bite or kick given the right conditions.

• Handling Problems

A horse must be handled often for routine care. If he behaves well while the following care is given, this indicates that he has been handled extensively by a knowledgeable trainer or owner, and probably has had good care. You certainly do not want a horse that requires sedation for shoeing, dental care or vet care, or that is difficult during routine grooming and handling chores. The best horse should:

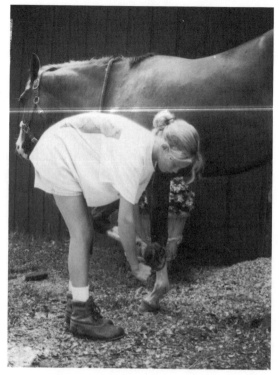

*Perform as many handling activities as
you can to spot bad behavior.*

- Stand still while being groomed, tacked up and mounted.

- Load into a trailer easily.

- Stand still while clipping his coat, even around his ears and fetlocks.

- Stand still for a farrier and vet.

- Stands quietly in cross ties.

- Stand quietly while being rinsed with water.

- Behave while someone is in his stall.

Try to perform as many of these handling activities as you can. You may have to rely on the answers that the seller gives you. These questions are listed in the questionnaire in the Appendix.

- Bucking and Rearing

Bucking and rearing are extremely tough habits to break, and obviously very dangerous. Once a horse has found out that he can dispose of his rider (and then probably not have to carry him again that day), he will try it again. Often the incident is not handled properly: the rider does not take control and continue to ride, instead the horse is put up and that teaches him how to end the riding session when he wants.

An experienced rider can handle a horse that is prone to buck. A horse can size up a rider quickly and some won't bother to buck if they are carrying an experienced rider.

A horse can buck to relieve an irritation. If his saddle pinches or he has saddle sores, his instinct will be to get that item off his back. Good quality and good fitting tack in good repair is essential.

Some horses will also buck when followed too closely by another horse on a trail or in the ring. Horses all move in their gaits at different speeds so it is difficult to pace a horse behind several others, especially for a beginning rider. This is more the fault of the rider than the horse, but some horses tolerate this better than others.

Horses rear to either unsettle their rider or because they are frightened.

*A martingale.*

One indication of a problem is the use of restrictive tack such as a martingale. The horse that requires such tack has not been trained properly and should be avoided by the beginning rider.

Bucking and rearing are like biting and kicking: you may not witness this during your inspection. Of course the more time you spend with the horse, and the more people you talk to about him increase your chances of knowing his true personality.

• Cribbing

"Cribbing" is the habit of gulping air which is difficult to break. The horse grips a vertical object such as a stall rail, braces his neck muscles so he can expand his esophagus and sucks air in. Some horses do it occasionally, while others seem addicted and obsessed. It is not known exactly why some horses start this, however it actually releases endorphins causing a pleasant sensation for the horse. Cribbing can cause health problems and is extremely difficult, if at all possible, to control. There are several commercial remedies such as collars and sprays that may work if used on a horse that has just started cribbing. The serious cribber, though, should be avoided. Other horses will learn to crib by watching.

*"Cribbing", even with a cribbing collar on.*

For more information on the issues related to owning a horse with a vice, read:

*The Problem Horse: An Owners Guide,* by Karen Bush, Howell Book House, 1992.

*There are no Problem Horses, Only Problem Riders,* by Mary Twelveponies, Houghton Mifflin Company, 1982 .

*Breaking Your Horse's Bad Habits*, by W. Dayton Sumner, Breakthrough Publications, Inc., 1986.

*Debugging Your Horse's Bad Habits,* by Bonnie Marlewski-Probert, K&B Products, 1-800-700-5096.

## GENERAL SIGNS OF HEALTH

A healthy horse will have a shiny coat, good feet and will act alert. An underweight condition is a good indication that the horse is in poor health, not wormed enough, has recently been ill, or his teeth have not been cared for. Don't be tempted to accept a horse that has a health problem or appears to have been neglected. If the horse is not healthy, this means he has also not been adequately ridden or trained recently. Nursing a neglected horse back to health requires an experts care and is not suitable for a first time owner. Rely on advice from a veterinarian to confirm the horse's health.

One serious condition that you must watch for is lameness. A horse that is lame does not carry his weight equally on all four legs, due to injury, disease or pain. There are several degrees of lameness, and not all preclude a horse from being a good riding partner. Though some horses can recover from the illness or injury and continue with a good career, you should avoid a horse that is obviously lame. There are several ways to observe lameness:

• Watch the horse trot from behind. His hindquarters should dip evenly as he trots.

• Watch from the side as he trots. His head should not bob when either leg hits the ground. If he is favoring a foreleg, his head will bob when the good leg hits the ground.

• Horses often rest a hind leg while standing, but it should not always be the same leg. They should periodically shift from leg to leg.

• A horse with good forelegs will never rest one with just the toe of the hoof on the ground. Both front hooves should be firmly planted on the ground.

• Look for obvious swelling. The forelegs should have the same shape and the hind legs should have the same shape. Swelling will not always indicate lameness, but should be checked by a vet.

## TRAINING

A highly trained animal means that an experienced trainer has invested many hours into the horse's discipline. This work adds dollars to the purchase price. A well trained horse is essential when considering safety and performance. High quality, consistent training can prevent or turn around bad habits.

A "green" horse is a horse that is newly broken but not schooled. The horse may have had a rider, but has not been trained sufficiently to deal with beginning riders. A horse is like a rider, needing consistent, high quality lessons and training by an experienced and gentle trainer. One of the worst mistakes is to buy a green horse for a beginner rider (a rider with less than 3 years of structured riding). This match is frustrating for both partners. An experienced horse with a good disposition, that can compensate for the poor skills of a beginning rider, and is more forgiving of mistakes will most certainly make a much better match for the new rider. A beginning rider on a green horse, however, can be an unpleasant and even dangerous combination. A green horse requires an experienced rider/trainer who can prevent bad habits from forming.

Though some horses can adapt well to changes in type of riding, it is best to find a horse that has been consistently ridden in the same way that you will ride him. For instance, if you intend to ride Western pleasure and trails, look for a horse that is currently ridden this way.

Every riding session is a training session for the horse, good or bad. If the rider is inexperienced, ongoing training and lessons will be a necessity to keep the horse well trained. Though opinions vary, if you choose a horse that is obviously more sophisticated than the rider, the horse will suffer. To retain his training, the horse needs the discipline and structure of an experienced rider. There are trainers who feel that you can never buy a horse that is too well trained no matter what the level of the rider. The rider may certainly learn and progress faster than if riding a green horse.

Be realistic when considering the training of the horse. Training a horse is not like training a dog. Only an experienced horse trainer can train a green horse. Choosing a foal, or a wild horse such as a mustang will be a tremendous disappointment, a large investment and usually ends up as a dilemma for the buyer, unless he is willing to pay for extensive training, and wait for many months to ride.

You can tell how well the horse is trained by watching the horse as it is being ridden. Watch as he carries a beginning rider, then as he carries an experienced rider. The well trained horse will move through his gaits and respond quickly to the riders signals. He will not hesitate or balk at the rider's signals. The well trained horse should respond well to the beginning rider also. An experienced rider can make most horses respond well. There are obvious signs you can watch for: refuses fences, difficult to stop, unwilling to go through his gaits. After you see a few horses, you will be able to see a difference. You may want to enlist the help of an experienced rider or your trainer in judging a horse's abilities and his tolerance for carrying a beginning rider.

## AGE

A horse is at his riding prime from age 5 to age 17. A younger horse is unproved and has not had the benefit of years of training. Your chances of getting a horse that is under age 5 with enough solid training is slim. Younger horses may not be as patient with an inexperienced rider and they are quicker to pick up bad habits than an old horse that is "set in his ways". However, a younger horse is more readily re-trained out of bad habits whereas the older horse may have difficulty learning new behavior.

The older horse, though often a fully acceptable riding partner, may require more health care. Resale value will be lower on an older horse because he is closer to the end of his riding career.

Age reflects not only the number of productive years left, but also the number of years of experience and training. Depending on training, care and health, most riding horses reach peak value at about age 10, and can be ridden until the day they die. At age 10 a horse is proven (good or bad), and still has many good years of riding ahead.

A horse younger than 5 will probably require more frequent riding. Just as younger people are more active, so are younger horses.

*This pony has reached the age of 37 due to the consistent loving care of his owners.*

## GELDING, STALLION OR MARE

Stallions are generally unacceptable as riding horses. They are hard to manage and dangerous. Most barns will not accept a stallion boarder. If you plan to keep your horse on your property, a stallion will require more substantial fencing and structures than a gelding or mare. Stallions, by nature, will want to rule the herd. In the domestic horse world, most males are neutered ("gelded") and most mares are not. Mares can be neutered but this is costly and they may require hormonal supplements. A stallion near a mare in season is dangerous - for handlers and other horses. Stallions should be on breeding farms specifically for breeding purposes only.

Geldings are neutered stallions and are the most desired for general riding. Even though geldings are castrated, some can retain the capability of mounting a mare which can be dangerous to both mare and gelding. Though pregnancy is highly unlikely, the chance of infection and injury are not. Usually a gelding with this tendency is isolated from mares in season.

Some mares can be just as quiet as geldings but may be difficult during estrous. Estrous occurs about every 28 days but is more prominent in the spring. A mare in season can be more apt to bite and kick other horses and people. She may also not perform as well, and not respond to her rider as well. In extreme cases, a mare in estrous will have to be isolated from other horses and may not be ridable. In the Spring, especially if showing, a hormonal implant is available which can lessen the symptoms of estrous. This is highly recommended. There is no difference in size between mares and geldings.

## SIZE

Sometimes size can affect the price of a horse. Height of over 16 hands will add substantially to the price. Also, a smaller show quality pony can be quite valuable.

The term "pony" is used to describe a horse that is 14 hands 2 inches and under. A "hand" is 4 inches, so a "pony" is any full grown horse standing 62 inches or less. This height is measured at the withers, which is the highest part of the back where the mane starts. A pony that stands at 14 hands is much larger than most people's idea of a pony. Generally a child shorter than 5 feet tall and weighing less than 80 pounds should be riding a pony. Although most adults should ride horses, a pony is appropriate for a small, beginning adult.

Be careful if you are considering a very small pony for a child. Small ponies can tend to have bad temperaments or bad habits. This is perhaps because a small pony is typically ridden by a small, young, inexperienced and immature rider. By the time the rider has matured into a good handler, he/she has outgrown that pony, who now has a new immature rider. This is not to say that all ponies should be avoided. On the contrary, a pony between 12 and 14 hands that is well trained, has a good way of going, and great temperament is an excellent find for an older child or small adult. A good pony of this size can carry a child for several years and has excellent resale value.

A small adult or child, who is an exceptional rider, can ride a large horse. Strength does not influence a horse to move to the riders commands, rather, it is the rider's subtle and experienced movements. Even the strongest man could not physically stop a small horse from bolting, but a small woman who is an experienced equestrian can command the attention and respect of the largest horse. Horses are controlled through training and good care. A reason you may not want to purchase a large animal for a small rider is that the pair may look out of balance in the show ring.

## WAY OF GOING

A horse with an excellent way of going will place in shows and will be a comfortable and beautiful riding horse. A horse can have great conformation and breeding, but if he doesn't move well, he will not be a successful riding partner. "Way of Going" refers to the smoothness of the gaits of a horse. This is most important for the show animal.

Watch him from the front, back and sides as someone else rides. His gaits (walk, trot and canter) should be smooth and the transition between gaits should be smooth. The intended rider should ride him to judge his way of going from the way the gaits feel from the saddle.

A horse can have a certain way of going that is good for one discipline but undesirable for another. For example, a short strided horse is desirable for Western equitation while a long strided horse is more desirable for the hunter ring. Your ability to judge this will improve after you have seen and compared several animals.

Conformation, health, fatigue, muscle strength, saddle, bridle, bit, quality of the feet and shoes, training and the experience of the rider all can affect way of going.

## Conformation

Sound conformation can add to a horse's beauty, balance, way of going and health. A horse with great conformation will have "curb appeal" and will have more potential buyers than one that is imperfectly proportioned, and therefore will command a higher price.

Conformation is the structure of the skeletal frame and musculature of the horse, and how proportional each part is to the whole. Put simply, conformation is how the horse is put together. If he is put together well he will jump better, handle better and have more endurance.

Conformation is important to the aesthetic look of the horse and also to the soundness, ability and performance of the horse. A horse that is put together well usually will move better, be more balanced, more powerful, and pleasing to look at. On the other hand, many horses with conformational faults perform well. For instance, San Lucas of the U.S. Olympic team was cow-hocked and ewe-necked Nautical was an outstanding show jumper. A horse with a conformational fault who also has great temperament, talent and heart is much more valuable than the horse with flawless conformation and a bad attitude.

If poor conformation contributes to a physical limitation or disability, it can also affect the horse's temperament. Just as some conformational faults are caused by incorrect shoes or tack, some can be corrected by proper tack, a good farrier and/or trainer.

Some conformational faults may only matter if the horse is ridden in a certain way. For instance a conformation fault may eliminate a horse from becoming a great jumper, but that same horse may prove to be an excellent dressage partner. Your vet and trainer can help you decide if a particular fault will have a negative impact on your riding discipline.

Conformation is a complex subject. Many experts disagree on some aspects of conformation and on the importance of "good" conformation. Experts also disagree as to the impact of conformation on the horse's performance. You can find more in depth discussion of conformation in text books, or in journal articles devoted to the subject. In selecting a horse, conformation should be considered but should not be a deciding factor.

## SHOW EXPERIENCE AND PLACEMENT

Of course, a winning record in respected shows adds credibility and value to a horse. Competition can vary tremendously from local 4H or Pony Club shows to the international show ring circuit. The value of the winning record will depend on the level of competition.

Some horses are natural competitors and shine in the show ring. Other horses, though terrific riding partners, do not perform well under the stress of travel and a new environment with strange people and other horses. If showing is intended for the new horse, a show record is valuable proof of his performance. If showing is not in the rider's interests, then show experience would needlessly add to the purchase price of the horse.

## COLOR

Flashy color can add to the price of a horse, although it should not be a deciding factor when selecting a horse. If you are dead set on an unusual color, you will have a much smaller selection to choose from. You may pass up a great buy waiting for a flashy color. The inexperienced rider, most often a child, can fall in love with a horse based on color. Horses bred for color (appaloosas, palominos and paints) are bred primarily for that reason so other qualities such as temperament, ability, and performance may suffer. Temperament, not color, should be the deciding factor in choosing a horse.

Color has an impact if you are showing in a particular class of riders. For instance, blacks, bays, chestnuts, grays (includes white) and paints are acceptable as hunt seat show horses. Loudly colored appaloosas are unacceptable for hunt seat showing but perfectly acceptable for Western riding. Palominos, buckskins and roans are acceptable in hunt seat shows if they have a good way of going. These general rules may vary depending on trend and location. A pretty color can sometimes be a positive factor the show ring.

# EVALUATING EACH HORSE

ow that you know what you are looking for, and how to find horses, you must go through the process of judging each candidate. Use these tips to weed out the best and the worst:

## AVOID BUYING A HORSE AS A SURPRISE

Try not to buy for a birthday or other timed event - this means you must choose from what is available at the time. Instead, give him this book on that day then include the rider in the selection process. Be sure to tell the rider that the selection process will take weeks or months. This can be a great opportunity for a parent to become involved in their child's passion for horses.

Unless the rider is extremely young and inexperienced (in which case he/she is not ready for horse ownership), be sure that he/she is involved in the search. What you think is right for them may be not their dream horse. You are making an important purchase. This horse will occupy a great deal of the rider's time for years to come and this decision could make or break the rider's drive to become an accomplished rider.

## USING A BROKER OR CONSULTANT

It takes years of daily work with horses to gain the knowledge necessary to evaluate a horse. You should involve an expert as a broker or a consultant in your search for the perfect horse. Ideally, the broker/consultant will be your instructor or trainer. Expect to pay for his time and expertise. This will cost you a few hundred dollars, but will vastly improve the chances that your selection is sound and safe.

A broker will find suitable horses and negotiate the sale. The broker's fee will be calculated in the price. The broker will want a percentage or a flat fee for the sale. In this arrangement, you will have less involvement in the selection or evaluation of the horse. You will have to trust that your broker is selecting a horse based on your needs, not on the fee for himself. In other words, if you negotiate a flat fee with the broker, he may try to find a horse as quickly as possible. Or, if the fee is based on a percentage of the purchase price, he may pass up less expensive but perfectly suitable horses for one that is highly priced.

An alternative to a broker is a consultant. This will probably be your instructor or trainer. Expect to pay him/her an hourly rate of $25 - $75. This could be expensive if you leave all the work to the consultant. To make the best use of this time, arrange an initial meeting with the consultant to discuss basic requirements. Read this book fully and be prepared. With his/her help, list requirements in order of importance, from "Must Have" to "Nice to Have". Go over the Questionnaire for Evaluating a Horse in the Appendix and add any questions that the consultant recommends that may be specific to your riding discipline or geographic area. Then you can provide the initial screening and search of horses through the sources listed above. Ask enough questions over the phone to know whether or not the horse is a possibility. Even if the horse is not exactly what you are looking for, or priced over your budget, you may want to see him for comparison to other horses.

Arrange visits to see the horses you have screened from phone calls. See the horses first yourself, and narrow the possibilities down to 5-6. Then have your consultant call the sellers and ask a few more questions. He/she may be able to eliminate one or two with a phone call rather than a visit. Then you and the consultant should make a second visit to see the horses that made the final cut.

A great way to narrow the search and use the consultant's time wisely is to use videos. Take someone

**137**

with you on the initial visits who can take a 10 minute video of each horse with the intended rider. Include a few minutes of the horse without tack and from all sides. Have the consultant review the tape. He/she will not be able to select a horse this way, but they can rule out one or two horses in a few minutes rather than spending hours on actual visits. Otherwise, you will be paying them for travel time, and any delays during the visit which can add up. Each visit to see a horse can take several hours. With this level of planning, you can get the most out of a few hours of an expert's time.

## THE EVALUATION

• Look him over

Look closely at the horse from all sides before he is tacked up. Run your hand down his legs and look for signs of previous injuries. Look and feel for swelling by comparing one limb to the other. Every horse will have some scars, but if you see a particularly large one, ask the seller to explain it's cause.

• See it All

Tell the seller that you want to see the horse being tacked up. Better yet, tack him up yourself. Watch and participate in as many handling situations as practical. Try to see the horse during more than one time of the day: morning, before and after feeding, at rest and after extensive exercise. The more activities you see, the better your chance of evaluating his temperament and witnessing bad habits such as biting, kicking, rearing or bucking.

• Ride and Watch

Watch as someone else rides the horse, and have the future owner ride him. Bring a friend, preferably someone with an equestrian background who can take pictures or videos of the rides. Watch the videos and compare.

If you intend to trail ride, see if the owner will let you test him on the trail. If you plan to jump, be sure to take him over fences. Whatever activities you have planned for your horse, test them out now. Take him through all of his gaits, several times. You may find a horse that is an exceptional show prospect, but dismal on the trail. This would be disappointing if trail riding is one of your favorite riding activities.

Refer to the previous chapter section "General Signs of Health" for signs of lameness.

• Strip out the setting and fancy tack

Try not to favor a horse that is shown in a gorgeous setting over the one that is ridden in a back yard paddock.

That one in the back yard paddock may be the better horse and probably will be priced lower. Overlook weather or other factors that may make the horse look better or worse than he is. If you ride a horse on a beautiful Spring day and another on a cold raining morning, you will remember the more pleasant ride and associate it with the horse. Be sure to give each horse equal time.

An expensive setting does not mean that a horse has had exceptional care. Expensive tack and surroundings can not substitute for consistent loving care. Try to judge the level of attentive care that the horse has had from the owner over the previous years, not the amount of money spent on trappings. Great care and attention can dramatically affect a horse's temperament and willingness to please.

## COMPARING THE HORSE TO OTHER HORSES

• Gather facts, be organized and compare

Take a picture of a potential horse and attach it to the questionnaire in the appendix. Get as much information from the questionnaire as time will allow. Use the pictures and information to compare all the horses you have seen. Take videos if possible. After seeing several horses, you can easily confuse facts among horses. Rely on your written notes and pictures.

- See and ride several horses

It is not unusual to look at 20-30 horses before making a decision. In the meantime, what you learn about horses, barns, trainers, sellers, the market and the whole equestrian way of life will be invaluable. After you've seen several horses, you will start to form specific opinions about what qualities you are after and what type of horse is the best fit for the rider. You will also gain information on the relative values of horses and be able to spot a fair price. You can also use this time to research the best boarding facilities. Set a goal, for instance, that you will see 20 horses and take 3 months to do so before making a decision.

If you have only ridden a couple of different horses in the past, riding a variety of horses can be quite informative. You will be amazed at how differently horses can move and feel under saddle. You may find that you prefer the feel of a lean horse to that of a muscular, wide barreled horse. Or you may find that the gaits of a taller horse are more comfortable than those of a shorter horse. You will never know what your preferences are until you have ridden a variety of horses.

## KNOW YOUR PRICE AND REQUIREMENTS

Remember that the purchase price is small in comparison to the cost of ongoing care. Stick to your limit but don't be too reluctant to look at horses outside of the range. You may find a gem priced lower. Looking at higher priced animals will give you a basis for comparison.

Be flexible on qualities that may not affect the ridability of the horse such as color, size and breed, and be firm on more important qualities such as temperament, health and way of going. List all your requirements in order of importance.

## THE VET CHECK

If the horse looks to you to be generally healthy, not visibly lame, and seems to be a good fit for the rider, the next recommended step is to pay a veterinarian to "vet" the horse. It will cost about $100, but you will save money and heartache by avoiding an unhealthy or unsound horse. For more expensive horses, you may consider full X-rays and a more extensive exam. X-rays can be performed at the barn. You may be able to negotiate this fee with the seller. If the seller is convinced of the soundness of the horse, he may pay for the vet check. Use a vet of your choice, not his.

A vet can spot conditions that are not apparent, and can advise you on the value of the horse. This is a valuable opportunity to get expert advice, so be present at the vetting, and ask the vet questions. Prepare a list of questions and concerns for the vet prior to the visit.

Have the vet confirm the horse's age. Tell the vet what type of riding you intend to do, and he can tell you if the horse is appropriate. He cannot, however, comment on temperament or personality, unless he has treated the horse for a long period of time.

Note that the vet will give you a conservative report on the horse. He will point out faults that may or may not impact the way you intend to ride the horse. He may tell you that the horse is technically "lame" but there are many degrees of lameness. A horse that scores a 1 or 2 on a flexion test may not be suitable for jumping but may be perfectly acceptable as a pleasure horse. Your instructor and your trainer should be able to help you decide if a flaw is significant to your riding discipline. If you are looking for a show horse of perfect quality, and your budget allows, then you may want to wait until you find a perfectly sound horse.

# NEGOTIATING THE PURCHASE

f you have looked at enough horses and talked to enough people, by the time you have chosen your horse, you should have a fair indication of it's value. Now is the time to negotiate the purchase. Buying a horse is like any major purchase - use common sense. Here are a few tips:

## DEALING WITH THE SELLER

- Take your time

Give yourself time to absorb all the facts about the horse in comparison to the others you have seen. Go home and methodically compare your requirements to each horse's qualities. Do not buy a horse on the spot. Don't let the seller or anyone else influence you into buying a horse until you have thoroughly evaluated him against others. Know what you are looking for and find out what is on the market so you can converse on an equal basis with the seller.

- Don't fall for typical sales lines

This is a transaction between 2 people and there is psychology involved. Don't act over anxious. Do not leave the seller with the indication that this is the best horse you have seen. Walk away and think about the horse for a day or two before you offer. Don't fall for the line, "there's another buyer interested in this horse and is prepared to buy." This is a ploy to get you to make a hasty decision, or to get full asking price.

Resist the urge to bring a horse trailer to the first visit to see a horse. If you absolutely fall in love with a horse and think that the price is exceptional, put a deposit down (make sure that it is refundable on your terms *in writing*), but still go home and sleep on it.

- Leave the seller with your name and phone number

If the seller calls you back, you can bet that he is motivated to sell, even if he says that someone else is prepared to buy the horse.

- Consider seller motivation

Ask why the horse is being sold. You may not get an honest answer, but when you compare his answers to the answers from others (other boarders, previous owners, trainers) you may find inconsistencies that you should investigate.

Be suspicious of a horse that seems to be extremely underpriced. His owner may be trying to dispose of him quickly. There may be a legitimate reason, such as the owner is relocating and cannot take the horse. Spend extra time with the horse to rule out bad habits or health issues. In some cases, you may find a terrific horse that has had exceptional care, but the owners must sell him and are flexible on the price to find a great home for their beloved horse.

## NEGOTIATING THE PRICE

- Use the facts you have gathered

Try to evaluate all the factors that can affect the price of the horse, compared to horses of the same quality. You will be qualified to assess this after you have seen many horses. You can use this information to negotiate with the owner.

# NEGOTIATING THE PURCHASE

Buying a horse is unlike buying a car in that you typically will deal with only one individual (unless you intend to buy from a large established breeder), and there are no set guidelines for pricing. Your offer only has to be approved by the owner. There won't be any strict sales guidelines or sales managers to bargain with. You can negotiate on items such as tack, the vet check, transportation of the horse to your location, financing, a trial or lease, or boarding at the owners facility. If there are other horses of the same quality in the area priced lower you may have leverage to negotiate the price. You may be able to appeal to the owner's desire to find a good home for his horse. If the horse is priced at less than $600, and the owner is not concerned about his welfare, you may not be able to negotiate because he can sell the horse for slaughter for $500-$700.

- Time of year can affect prices

Prices will generally be higher in late Spring and early Summer. Sometimes prices are inflated for the Christmas season also.

- If the price is fair, take it

If you truly feel that this is the right horse and he is priced fairly, then offer the full price. Ultimately, your cost of caring for the horse are going to be much greater than this purchase price, so concentrate on getting the best horse, rather than dickering on the price. If the purchase price is over your budget, negotiate financing with the owner.

- Try to get a trial

You may be able to negotiate a trial period to evaluate the horse. A trial of 2 weeks to a month should be sufficient to evaluate the horse. The seller will want a deposit (which may or may not be refundable) and may not permit you to move the horse to another location. Whatever your verbal agreement is, be sure to get it in writing.

## THE BILL OF SALE

- Put Everything in Writing

Once you come to an agreement with the seller, you should put it in writing. Most people you deal with are going to be honest, but you still need to have a written agreement in case there is a misunderstanding. If you have arranged a trial, or lease, if the sale is contingent on a vet check, or if you offer a refundable deposit, or any other terms for payment, put it in writing and have the seller sign and date it. See "Leasing a Horse" in Section One for information leasing, and see the Appendix for a Sample Lease Contract.

Have a Bill of Sale ready and understand it. Look at the example in the Appendix. If the seller insists on using his, be sure you understand the terms fully before signing.

- Get proof of a negative Coggin's test

Be sure you have proof of a negative Coggin's test before signing a Bill of Sale. All states require a negative Coggin's test yearly and some states require a negative Coggin's within 6 months for interstate travel. In all states it is illegal to buy, sell or transport a horse without a current Coggin's test.

## TAKE ONE LAST REALITY CHECK

Take one more look at your original requirements and don't compromise on qualities that are important. Skim through the first section of this book and be sure that you are prepared for horse ownership.

Consider leasing one more time. Leasing a horse is a great alternative (or first step) to buying. By the time your lease is up, you will know if this is the horse for you (if he is for sale) or at least you will have a good idea of the qualities that you are looking for in a horse.

## BUYER BEWARE!

As far as the law is concerned, the buyer should beware. Sellers must tell the truth when asked. The seller may indicate truthfully that the horse does not have any known vices, but he cannot guarantee the horse's future behavior with another individual. The seller will probably not offer information on a bad habit or quality, so you must ask. Come right out and ask about the horse's habits and temperament. The seller may be more inclined to speak honestly if you have a witness.

After the Bill of Sale is signed, you should consider the sale final and the horse yours. Even if you feel that the seller misled you, your chances of reversing the sale are slim. Of course if the seller agrees to take back the horse, you are extremely lucky. Even if you win a lawsuit, court action is rarely successful because legal fees, time and heartache are substantial.

Avoid this by taking your time, thoroughly evaluating the horse as described above and asking many questions of many people who know the horse. Try to get a lease or trial period with the horse. Organized, analyzed information is your best tool to avoiding a problem horse. It will be much more pleasant to spend your time up front while selecting your horse rather than at the back end trying to get out of a bad deal.

# APPENDIX

# QUESTIONNAIRE FOR EVALUATING A HORSE

(Attach the ad and a picture of the horse to this questionnaire)

Name of HORSE:_____

Registry:_____Registration Number:_____

Sex:_____ HT:_____ Age:_____ Color:_____Breed:_____

MARKINGS:_____

Sellers Name:_____Phone: _____

Location of horse:_____Date of Inspection:_____

Asking Price:_____Negotiable?_____

Includes any tack, equipment, or transportation?_____

Date of last negative Coggin's:_____

Will Seller agree to a trial period or lease?_____

Why is the horse for sale?_____

How long has the seller had the horse?_____

Who was the previous owner?_____

Ask more than one person (such as the vet, farrier, previous owner, other owners at the barn) some of questions to see if the answers are consistent.

o  Who is his vet?_____

o  When were his teeth last floated?_____

o  Will he pass a vet test?_____

o  Last injury and how it occurred?_____

o  Has he ever been labeled as "lame"?_____

o  Does he appear lame now?_____

o  Has he ever had colic?_____

**154**

o Are vaccinations and worming current?_____

o Does he wear shoes, how many, does he have good feet?_____

o Who is his farrier?_____

o Does he have a special diet or require supplements?_____

o Is his coat shiny and even? Is it sufficiently thick if winter or thin if summer?

_____

o Is he alert, but not too skittish?_____

o Are his eyes clear?_____

o Are there any visible injuries, or scars from previous injuries?_____

Schooling, Experience and Way of Going

o What kind of rider is riding the horse now and what kind of experience does that

rider have?_____

o How much does he need to be ridden?_____

o How much is he ridden how?_____

o How is he ridden now: trails, shows, lessons, school horse, on the track?

_____

o Does he have a show record - where and in what company (local, state or nationally recognized association?

_____

o   Smoothness of gaits and transition from gait to gait

_____

o Responsiveness to riders signals

_____

Temperament and habits

Try to perform as much as you can, otherwise, ask the seller:

o Does he load into a trailer easily?_____

o Does he stand still when groomed?_____

o  Can you clean his hooves without trouble?_____

o  Does he stand still when tacking up or mounting?_____

o  Does he stand for the farrier?_____

o  Will he stand for clipping?_____

o  Does he stand in cross ties?_____

o  Has he been known to bite, kick, buck or rear?_____

o  Is he a cribber?_____

o  How is he with children (if applicable)?_____

o  How does he behave with other horses (if applicable)?_____

o  How is he with other animals (if applicable)?_____

o  Is there evidence in his stall of chewing or kicking rails?_____

o  Does he pin his ears while being handled? _____

o  Do you know of any bad habits or qualities that we have not already discussed?

_____

Other

o Does he look proportioned?

_____

o If a mare, how does she behave in estrous?

_____

o How much does he eat?

_____

o Does he require any feed supplements?

_____

**156**

# QUESTIONNAIRE FOR EVALUATING A BARN

Barn Owner:_____Phone:_____

Barn Manager:_____Phone_____

Location of Barn:_____

Date of Visit:_____Monthly Boarding Fee:_____

Includes or excludes:_____

General

o  Is the barn is reputable?  Visit the barn and talk to the owner and/or manager, and talk to current boarders.  Visit a tack store nearby and ask about the barn.

_____

o  Is the barn half full of boarders when other nearby barns are full?  If so, try to find out why.

_____

o  Is the barn overly crowded?  Many horses without their own stalls?  Overgrazed areas?

_____

o  Is the barn manager focused on quality care?  Is his/her personality acceptable?

_____

Condition of the Facilities

o  Are the buildings and fencing in good repair?_____

o  Is the riding ring large enough for comfortable lessons? _____

o  Is the surface of ring should be even and covered with a surface material such?  Is

it muddy or wet?_____

o  Is the ring lit for riding  the evening or early morning?_____

o  Is there an indoor ring?_____

o  Is the feed room clean and secure to reduce pests?_____

o  Is all tack should be put away in a tack room?_____
o  Is the tack room sufficient size and organized properly?_____

o  Is feed in a separate sheltered feed room?_____

o  Is there a wash room that has a concrete floor and easy access to water?_____

o  Are stalls clean with dry, fresh bedding?  Are the floor of the stalls dry and in good

condition? _____

o  Are stalls at least 10 by 10? _____

o  Are stall structures sturdy and in good repair?_____

o  Are flies and rodents under control?  (you will not find a barn that is completely free

from pests) without overuse of pesticides?_____

o  Is there a grass pasture with cross fencing?  Cross fencing allows the manager to

separate horses who do not get along into different sections._____

o  Is the hay dry, and without a musty odor?_____

o  Is the barn clean, clean, clean?_____

Care of the Horses

type of hay used_____

type of feed used_____

who is the vet _____

who is the farrier_____

o  Do most of the horses should look healthy (shiny coat, good weight, alert)?  If one or 2 horses do not look particularly healthy, ask the barn manager.  They may be newcomers who are being nursed back to health.

_____

o  Are all horses turned out DAILY?

Comments:_____

_____

_____

Services Offered

o  Are there plenty of scheduled activities and other horse owners and riders around?

_____

o  Is there a reputable resident trainer (horse trainer and riding instructor)?

_____

o  Are there varied lesson plans scheduled?_____

o  Are there summer camps for children and/or clinics for adults?_____

o  Does the barn participate in and/or sponsors shows?_____

_____

o  Is trailer transportation available?_____

## Sample Bill of Sale

The following is a sample Bill of Sale. You should consult an
attorney in your area specializing in equestrian issues to insure
that the Bill of Sale covers all issues related to your local laws
and your specific situation.

# Sample Bill of Sale

Name of HORSE:_____

Registry:_____Registration Number:_____

Sex:_____ HT:_____ Age:_____ Color:_____Breed:_____

MARKINGS:_____

Date of last negative Coggin's:_____

Purchase price: $_____. Down Payment: $_____. Balance to be paid in _____ months at $_____per month, due on the _____ day of the month.

The OWNER/SELLER will give the transfer of ownership to the BUYER upon completion of payment. The BUYER will pay the transfer fee.

If the above terms of payment are broken the BUYER will be held responsible for all legal expenses and fees that may be necessary to collect payment.

As of _____ all expenses/costs incurred by or for the above horse will be paid by_____.

To the best of the OWNERS/SELLERS knowledge, at the time of sale, the above horse is sound, in good health, and has not been known to cause injury to riders or handlers. The horse is sold "as is". Inspection by a veterinarian or farrier is the responsibility of the BUYER.

I hereby agree to the above terms and statements:

OWNER/SELLER:                    BUYER:

Signature_____Signature_____

Date_____Date_____

Name_____Name_____

Street_____Street_____

Witness_____

## SAMPLE ASSUMPTION OF LIABILITY STATEMENT

If you intend to allow others to ride your horse, you should have them sign an Assumption of Liability Statement. Mishaps can occur which can cause injury to the rider, other people or damage to property.

The following is a sample agreement. You should check with an attorney in your area specializing in equestrian issues to insure that the agreement covers all issues related to your local laws and your specific situation.

# SAMPLE ASSUMPTION OF LIABILITY STATEMENT

I assume and accept all liability for bodily injury and/or property damage that may result from my use, or the use by my minor child, of the horse named_____ (hereby referred to as "HORSE") belonging to _____(hereby referred to as "OWNER"). I agree to hold OWNER, his/her employees and all other participants other than myself harmless for any damages sustained to me, my minor child, any third party or property whatsoever relating to my use, or the use by my minor child of HORSE.

I understand that headgear approved by the American Horse Show Association can substantially reduce the risk of head injury and I agree to wear such headgear, or have my minor child wear such headgear, at all times while mounted on HORSE.

I further agree that in the event of a lawsuit, or any action against OWNER relating to my use, or the use by my minor child of HORSE, I will pay the OWNER's legal fees, and any court costs or damages which may accrue or for which may be ordered against OWNER.

I understand that HORSE has the following bad habits or peculiarities :_____

_____

I have read, understood, and will abide by the contents of the above agreement.

_____Date_____
Signature of Rider, or Legal Guardian/Parent of Rider

_____
Printed Name of Rider, or Legal Guardian/Parent of Rider

_____
Printed Name of Minor Child

# SAMPLE LEASE CONTRACT

The terms of a lease contract are highly variable. The contract is simply a statement of all terms that the leasee and owner agree to related to the temporary use of the horse. As a leasee, you will want to have enough freedom to ride the horse when, how and where you wish to. You want to be able to transport the horse to events, trails or shows. You may want to allow another person to ride the horse, or you may want exclusive rights to the horse. You may want to use certain tack. You need to know what expenses you are responsible for. And it must be very clear who is liable in the event of personal or property damage during the lease term.

The owner will want to insure that his horse and tack are properly cared for. He may wish to ride the horse during the lease period. He will want to insure that he is not liable for property or personal damages that occur during the lease period. He may not want his horse ridden in a certain way, such as on trails, or on the street. He may want a deposit on any tack that he loans. If the horse is highly valuable, both owner and leasee may want insurance coverage in case the horse is severely injured during the lease term.

If the leasee is to pay board directly to the barn owner, then the barn owner must be notified. The owner normally is under contract to the barn manager for feeding and boarding and this agreement must be modified if another individual is taking on the responsibility. It may be simpler and cleaner to include boarding costs in with the lease fee, and let the owner pay the barn manager according to the boarding contract. Preferably the barn manager should sign the lease contract as a witness and have a copy.

The following is a sample of common issues that need agreement between both parties. You should alter the contract to include any other details that you and the owner agree upon.

The following is a sample contract. You should check with an attorney in your area specializing in equestrian issues to insure that the contract covers all issues related to your local laws and your specific situation.

# Sample Lease Contract

Name of HORSE:_____

Registry:_____Registration Number:_____

Sex:_____ HT:_____ Age:_____ Color:_____Breed:_____

MARKINGS:_____

_____

The OWNER of the above named HORSE agrees to lease HORSE to LEASEE under the following terms and conditions:

Boarding location of HORSE during lease term:

_____

Lease term is from _____ (date) to_____ (date). LEASEE agrees to pay OWNER a fee of $_____ per month due on the _____day of each month. A late fee of $_____will be charged if payment is ____ days late. If payment is _____days late, this lease contract is null and void.

All feeding and boarding fees will be paid by LEASEE/OWNER (circle one).

LEASEE can ride HORSE at anytime with the exception of:

_____

Other persons who can ride HORSE during lease term:

_____

OWNER WILL/WILL NOT (circle one) have priority over usage of HORSE provided OWNER gives LEASEE _____days notice. If OWNER rides HORSE for more than ____ days in any month, OWNER will deduct $_____per day from the next month's lease fee. OWNER can ride HORSE a maximum of _____days per month.

During lease period, LEASEE will carry liability insurance in the amount of $_____. Any personal injury, damage to property, or injury to HORSE that occurs during lease period will be the sole responsibility of LEASEE.

LEASEE may use the following tack owned by OWNER provided that tack is cleaned, stored properly and kept in good repair:

Item:_____Market Value:_____

Item:_____Market Value:_____

**166**

If tacked listed above is damaged, lost or stolen during term of lease, LEASEE will pay OWNER the Market Value as listed above upon termination of lease.

LEASEE MAY/MAY NOT (circle one) transport HORSE to:

_____

_____

LEASEE is responsible for all transportation fees during lease period, including transportation to and from boarding location of lease term.

LEASEE is responsible for all veterinary fees, emergency as well as routine, incurred during lease term. The only routine, non-emergency veterinary fees that will be incurred during lease term are:

_____

_____

LEASEE is responsible for all farrier fees incurred during lease term. LEASEE will have HORSE shod by _____(farrier) at least once every _____months.

This lease may be canceled at any time by either LEASEE or OWNER.

LEASEE understands that HORSE has the following bad habits or peculiarities:

_____

_____

LEASEE, and any other persons who are listed above as riders, agree to sign an Assumption of Liability Statement.

I UNDERSTAND AND AGREE TO ALL THE TERMS AND CONDITIONS OF THIS LEASE CONTRACT:

OWNER:                          LEASEE:

Signature_____Signature_____

Date_____Date_____

Name_____Name_____

Street_____Street_____

Barn Manager_____

**167**

# Sample Boarding Agreement

Add to the following standard boarding agreement any additional provisions that are agreed upon between owner and barn manager such as:

- agreement to use horse as school horse, how many times per week, who can and cannot ride him, how he can or cannot be ridden, whether or not he can be trailered to shows, trails or events, use of the owners tack for schooling

- supplemental feedings, special hay or feed, special vitamins, dressing wounds, special health care

- how he should be turned out (for example, only in morning or evening, only where there is shade, not in the woods, not with certain other horses, with or without halter)

- which stall he will have, no other horse will use that stall

- exchange of work for partial payment of board

The following is a sample agreement. You should check with an attorney in your area specializing in equestrian issues to insure that the agreement covers all issues related to your local laws and your specific situation.

# Sample Boarding Agreement

Name of HORSE:_____

Registry:_____Registration Number:_____

Sex:_____ HT:_____ Age:_____ Color:_____Breed:_____

MARKINGS:_____

_____

Barn agrees to provide stall, daily cleaning of stall, daily turnout, water, grain and hay twice daily, for $____/month to be paid in advance on the _____ of the month. If fee is not paid within 30 days of due date a late fee of $_____will be charged. If fee has not been paid for 90 days a lien may be placed on the horse by _____.

The OWNER(S) agree not to hold BARN, its agents or anyone in its employ liable for any illness, injury, death or loss of the horse, person or property.

The OWNER(S) agree to pay all professional fees incurred for veterinary and farrier care. The veterinarian to be used shall be _____. If this veterinarian is not available

_____ shall be called. In the case of emergency (as evaluated by the Barn manager) if neither of these veterinarians is available the manager or her representative may call the veterinarian of her choice. Non-emergency care will be discussed with the OWNER(S) in advance.

The farrier will be _____ unless he is not available, in which case the manager or her representative may use the farrier of her choice. Shoeing/trimming will be discussed with the OWNER(S) in advance.

The horse will not be removed for any reason without permission of the OWNER(S) nor will the OWNER(S) remove the horse without prior notification to the manager. The only exception to this will be if the horse must be taken for emergency veterinary care.

OWNER(S):                          BARN:

Name:_____        _____

Address:_____        _____

Phone: _____        _____

DATE:_____        _____

# EQUESTRIAN JOURNALS AND MAGAZINES

## APPALOOSA JOURNAL

Means of communication of the Appaloosa Horse Club. Aimed towards Appaloosa enthusiasts around the world. Includes horse and rider success stories, and trends in breeding, training and marketing. Monthly, $20/Year. Circulation 15,455.

Appaloosa Horse Club   (208)882-5578
Box 8403
Moscow, ID 83843

## ARABIAN HORSE WORLD

Aimed towards owners, breeders and admirers of the Arabian breed. Stories cover Arabians past and present, in America and abroad. Articles on healthcare and performance. Events covered include national Championships, clinics, shows, sales and Arabian Association activities. Monthly, $40/Year. Circulation: 11,000.

Arabian Horse World   (415)856-0500
824 San Antonio Ave.
Palo Alto, CA 94303

http://www.ahwmagazine.com

## THE CHRONICLE OF THE HORSE

Official publication of :   U.S. Equestrian Team, U.S. Dressage Team, Masters of Foxhounds Association of America, Roster of Packs of the Nat'l Beagle Club, U.S. Pony Club, Inc., American Foxhound Club, Nat'l Riding Committee of the American Alliance of Health, Physical Education, Recreation and Dance American Vaulting Association.

News and results of horse shows and events.   Riding tips and horse care information.   Weekly, $47/year.   Circulation: 21,000.

Chronicle of the Horse  (540)687-6341
Box 46
301 W Washington St.
Middleburg, VA  22018

## EQUUS

Articles and features on horse care, veterinary research, performance, training, riding, stable management, and consumer opportunities. Monthly, $24/year. Circulation: 145,532.

Equus  (301)-977-3900
656 Quince Orchard Rd
Ste 600
Gaithersburg, MD  20878

**170**

## HORSE & RIDER

Aimed towards the western rider who seeks to improve skills and style in the show ring. Articles and features include detailed riding instruction, profiles of top winners, consumer advice on equine products, western fashion trends and accessories. Monthly, $19.95/year. Circulation: 173,758.

Horse & Rider  (303)914-3000
12265 W Bayaud,  Ste 300
Lakewood, CA  80228

## HORSE AND HORSEMAN

Western and English disciplines. How-to articles on training, breeding, feeding, and riding for pleasure or show. Special issues devoted to topics such as horse health or management, and equestrian products. Monthly, $18/year. Circulation: 77,882.

Horse and Horseman  (714)493-2101
34249 Camino Capistrano
Box HH
Capistrano Beach, CA  92624

## HORSE ILLUSTRATED

For horse owners, both English and Western. Articles on health care and performance. Regular features on showing, training, conditioning, feeding, and care with an emphasis on showing. Monthly, $23.97/year. Circulation: 186,375.

Horse Illustrated  (213)385-2222
2410 Beverly blvd.
Los Angeles, CA 90057

## HORSE SHOW

Published by the American Horse Show Association. Focuses on rules, regulations and policies that govern the AHSA. Articles and interviews on judging, veterinary medicine, management, and training. Profiles of leading riders. Competition calendar.
10 issues/yr. Circulation: 58,500.

Horse Show  (212)972-2472
220 E 42nd St
Ste 409
New York, NY  10017

## PAINT HORSE JOURNAL

Published by the American Paint Horse Association. Content includes Paint horse breeding, showing, racing, training, consumer product review, trail riding and packing. Monthly, $26/year. Circulation: 20,747.

Paint Horse Journal   (817)439-3400
Box 961023
Fort Worth, TX 76161

## PRACTICAL HORSEMAN

How-to journal for English riders.  Articles include breeding, raising, training, health care, stable management, veterinary research, money and time saving tips, personal interviews with top riders. Monthly, $24.95/year.  Circulation: 90,754.

Practical Horseman  (717)657-9555
6405 Flank Drive
Harrisburg, PA 17112

## THE QUARTER HORSE JOURNAL

Published by the American Quarter Horse Association. Factual articles of interest to those who own, breed, train and show AQHA registered horses.  Includes training, veterinary issues, equine research, youth activities, show reports, sales information.
Monthly,  $25/year. Circulation: 72,737.

The Quarter Horse Journal  (806)376-4888
1600 Quarter Horse Drive
Amarillo, TX  79168

## THE WESTERN HORSE

Emphasis on Western style of riding.  Content includes nutrition, care and grooming, breeding, training, general health care, western fashion trends. Monthly,  $18/year. Circulation: 81,530.

The Western Horse  (619)788-1427
2493 Montcecito Rd
Ramona CA, 92065

## WESTERN HORSEMAN

General interest horse magazine with emphasis on Western style riding.  Articles cover ranching, rodeo, profiles of horse and riders, health care, gear,  Western historical stories, poems, humor, trail riding stories.  Monthly, $20/year. Circulation: 228,555.

Western Horseman  (719)633-5524
Box 7980
3850 N Nevada Ave
Colorado Springs, CO 80933

# EQUESTRIAN ASSOCIATIONS

Below is a listing of Equestrian Associations that have more than 5,000 members. Many of these associations offer newsletters, journals, insurance, conferences, shows and other benefits.

### AMERICAN BUCKSKIN REGISTRY ASSOCIATION
P.O. Box 3850
Redding, CA 96049-3850
(916)223-1420     5,500 members

### AMERICAN EQUINE ASSOCIATION
Box 658
Newfoundland, NJ 07435
(201)697-9668     56,000 members

### AMERICAN HORSE SHOWS ASSOCIATION
220 E. 42nd St. Ste 409
New York, NY 10017-5876
(212)972-2472     60,000 members

### AMERICAN MORGAN HORSE ASSOCIATION
Box 960
Shelburne, VT 05482
(802)985-4944     11,500 members

### AMERICAN PAINT HORSE ASSOCIATION
Box 961023
Fort Worth, TX 76161
(817)439-3400     48,089 members

### AMERICAN QUARTER HORSE ASSOCIATION
1600 Quarter Horse Dr.
Amarillo, TX 79104
(806)-376-4811     288,000 members

### AMERICAN QUARTER HORSE YOUTH ASSOCIATION
1600 QuarterHorse Dr.
Box 200
Amarillo, TX 79104

(806)376-4888    31,000 members

## AMERICAN QUARTER PONY ASSOCIATION
New Sharon, IA  50207
(515)675-3669    5,000 members

## AMERICAN SADDLEBRED HORSE ASSOCIATION
c/o The Kentucky Horse Park
4093 Iron Works Pike
Lexington, KY 40511
(606)259-2742    7,300 members

## AMERICAN SHETLAND PONY CLUB
6748 N Frostwood Pkwy
Peoria, IL  61615
(309)691-9661    5,500 members

## APPALOOSA HORSE CLUB
Box 8403
Moscow, ID  83843
(208)882-5578    26,000 members

## ARABIAN HORSE REGISTRY OF AMERICA
12000 Zuni St.
Westminster, CO  80234
(303)450-4748    22,000 members

## BELGIAN DRAFT HORSE CORPORATION OF AMERICA
Box 335
Wabash, IN  46992
(219)563-3205    5,500 members

## INTERCOLLEGIATE HORSE SHOW ASSOCIATION
Smoke Run Farm
Hollow Rd Box 741
Stony Brook, NY  11790
(516)751-2803    5,000 members

## INTERNATIONAL ARABIAN HORSE ASSOCIATION
Box 33696
Denver, CO  80233
(303)450-4774    30,000 members

**174**

## MISSOURI FOX TROTTING HORSE BREED ASSOCIATION

Box 1027
Ava, MO 65608
(417)683-2468     5,500 members

## NATIONAL CUTTING HORSE ASSOCIATION

4704 Hwy. 377 S.
Fort Worth, TX 76116
(817)244-6188     10,800 members

## NATIONAL REINING HORSE ASSOCIATION

448 Main St. Ste 204
Coshocton, OH 43812
(614)623-0050     7,000 members

## NATIONAL SHOW HORSE REGISTRY

11700 Commonwealth Dr. Ste 200
Louisville, KY 40299
(502)266-5100     5,500 members

## PALOMINO HORSE BREEDERS OF AMERICA

15253 E Skelly Dr.
Tulsa, OK 74116-2637
(918)438-1234     10,135 members

## PASO FINO HORSE ASSOCIATION

101 N. Collins St.
Plant City, FL 33566-3311
(813)719-7777          5,162 members

## PINTO HORSE ASSOCIATION OF AMERICA

1900 Samuels Ave.
Fort Worth, TX 76102
(817)336-7842     6,000 members

## UNITED STATES COMBINED TRAINING ASSOCIATION

Box 2247
Leesburg, VA 22075
(703)779-0440     10,500 members

## UNITED STATED DRESSAGE FEDERATION

Box 80668
Lincoln, NE 68501
(402)434-8550    30,000 members

## UNITED STATES EQUESTRIAN TEAM

Gladstone, NJ 07934
(908)234-1251    25,000 members

## UNITED STATES PONY CLUBS

c/o The Kentucky Horse Park
4071 Iron Works Pike
Lexington, KY 40511
(606)254-7669    12,000 members

## TENNESSEE WALKING HORSE BREEDERS' AND EXHIBITORS ASSOCIATION

Box 286
Lewisburg TN 37091
(615) 359-1574  5,800 members

# REFERENCES

Ambrosiano, Nancy and Harcourt, Mary. *Complete Plans for Building Horse Barns Big and Small.* 1989, Breakthrough.

Bush, Karen. *The Problem Horse: An Owners Guide.* 1992, Howell Book House.

Clemens, Virginia Phelps. *A Horse in Your Backyard.* 1991, Prentice Hall Press

Eley, Janet. *Understanding Your Horse's Health.* 1992, Ward Jack Ltd., 1992.

Eustis-Cross, Barbara and Bowker, Nancy. *The Wild Horse: An Adopter's Manual.* 1992, Howell Book House.

Gale Research: *Encyclopedia of Associations,* 31st ed. 1996.

Hawcroft, Tim. *The Complete Book of Horse Care.* 1991, Howell Book House.

Hill, Cherry. *Horsekeeping on a Small Acreage.* 1990, Storey Communications, Inc.

Marlewski-Probert, Bonnie. *Debugging Your Horse's Bad Habits.* K&B Products, 1-800-700-5096.

Metter, John J. Jr. *Horse Sense.* 1989, Garden Way Publishing.

Mills, Bruce and Carne, Barbara. *A Basic Guide to Horse Care and Management.* 1988, Howell Book House, Inc.

Pets Forum Group, Inc. *Horses Forum.* 1996 via CompuServe.

Smith Sharon B. *The Affordable Horse.* 1994, Howell Book House.

SRDS. *SRDS Consumer Magazine Advertising Source.* July, 1996, Vol. 78 #7.

Stoneridge, M.A. *A Horse of Your Own.* 1990, Doubleday.

Stoneridge, M.A. *Practical Horseman's Book of Horsekeeping.* 1983, Doubleday.

Strickland, Charlene. *Tack Buyer's Guide .* 1988, Breakthrough Publications, Inc.

Sumner, W. Dayton. *Breaking Your Horse's Bad Habits .* 1986, Breakthrough Publications, Inc.

Twelveponies, Mary. *There are no Problem Horses, Only Problem Riders.* 1982, Houghton Mifflin Company.

# GLOSSARY

**Back at the knee**
A conformational fault in which the foreleg is bowed backwards at the knee.

**Bay**
A color of horse. Black mane and tail, black lower legs, and reddish brown over the rest of the body.

**Bedding**
Wood shavings, shredded newspaper, straw, sand or other materials used to line the floor of a stall.

**Bit**
Metal bar on a bridle that goes in the horses mouth and is used to control the horse while riding.

**Blaze**
a broad white stripe down the face

**Bowed hocks**
A conformational fault in which the hocks on the hind legs are turned too far outwards.

**Bowed tendon**
a permanently swollen tendon. Does not result in lameness but tendon will not be as strong.

**Breed**
A distinct genetic entity. Recognized members of a breed are entered in an official stud book.

**Brown**
A color of horse, with a mixture of black and brown hairs on the body and black points.

**Bucking**
A vice in which the horse kicks out his back legs, both at the same time, usually to unsettled the rider or rid himself of irritating tack.

**Canter**
One of the four natural gaits of a horse. Slower than a gallop, this is a three beat gait.

**Chestnut**
A color of horse, reddish brown with a similar colored mane and tail, or the bony protrusion on the inside of forearm of each foreleg.

178

**Cob**     A small, strong horse descended from draft horses. About 15 hands high.

**Colt**     A male horse under 3 years old.

**Combined Training**     Also called "Three Day Eventing", an English style of riding competition which includes dressage, stadium jumping and a cross-country course.

**Conformation**     The build of a horse, the way he is put together. A horse with good conformation will look proportional.

**Coronet**     Surface of the hoof

**Cow hocks**     A conformational fault in which the hocks on the hind legs are turned inward towards each other.

**Cribbing**     A vice in which the horse grabs onto a horizontal object, stretches his esophagus and sucks wind. This behavior is learned and can range from occasional to obsessive.

**Curb**     thickening of the ligament on the back of the hind leg. May or may not result in lameness.

**Curb bit**     A single-bar mouthpiece that is attached at each end to upright bars (as compared to rings on a snaffle bit). These bits give more control but are not as gentle on a horse's mouth as a snaffle bit. They are usually used in Polo and Western riding disciplines.

**Curry comb**     A plastic or rubber comb with several rows of short flexible bristles. Used for removing loose hair and dirt.

**Dam**     The mother of a horse.

**Dock**     The area at the top of the tail.

**Dorsal stripe**     a dark stripe along a horse's back. Common on early horses and seen today on some buck skin or other dark skinned horses.

**Dun**     A color of horse. Light to medium sand colored with dark skin. Usually has dark points (mane, tail and lower legs.)

**English**     A style of riding that includes many sports such as dressage, racing, jumping, combined training, saddle seat, trail, pleasure and more. Characterized by a saddle that is smaller and plainer than a Western saddle with no large pommel to test your hands. The rider holds a rein in each hand and steers the horse by gently pulling on the rein on the right rein to turn right, or the left to turn left.

**179**

| | |
|---|---|
| **Eohippus** | small (14"), earliest ancestor of the modern day horse. |
| **Farrier** | A professional who shoes horses. |
| **Feathers** | The long hairs of the fetlock that cover the hooves of some draft horses. |
| **Fetlock** | The "ankle" joint of each leg. |
| **Filly** | A female horse under 3 years old. |
| **Foal** | A male or female under a year old. |
| **Frog** | The fleshy triangular underside of the hoof. |
| **Gait** | The four different ways a horse can move: walk, trot, canter and gallop. |
| **Gallop** | The fastest of the four natural gaits of a horse. This is a four beat gait. |
| **Gelding** | A male horse that has been castrated. |
| **Grade Horse** | A horse with a mixture of breeds in his ancestry. |
| **Gray** | A color of horse that ranges from white to dark gray. Includes dapple. All grays have black skin. |
| **Green** | Used to describe a horse that has had a rider but is in the early stages of training. |
| **Halter** | A harness of leather, rope or nylon that fits over a horse's head. This is much like a bridle without the bit or reins. It is used for leading a horse. |
| **Hand** | A hand is 4 inches. Height is measured at the withers, the highest point on a horse's back just before his mane starts. |
| **Hock** | The "knee" of the hind legs. |
| **Hoof pick** | A metal or strong plastic tool with a pointed end for picking debris out of the underside of hooves. |
| **Horn** | the surface of the hoof. Horns can be pale, dark or mixed, and all colors are similar in hardness. |
| **Lame** | A condition in which a horse does not carry weight equally on all four legs, due to disease or injury. |

**180**

| | |
|---|---|
| **Laminitis** | inflammation of the laminae (the inside lining of the hoof) |
| **Lead change** | The "lead" is the foreleg of the horse that is farthest in front during a canter. A good rider can signal the horse to change his lead. |
| **Mare** | An adult female horse. |
| **Martingale** | A leather strap that goes from the girth to the bridle underneath the chin which prevents a horse from throwing his head up. |
| **Mucking a stall** | Cleaning out the manure and soiled bedding in a stall. |
| **Navicular disease** | A disease of the navicular bone (a small bone at the end of the leg) which leads to lameness. Caused by improper shoeing and excess stress on the hooves. |
| **Over at the knee** | A conformational fault in which the foreleg is bowed forward at the knee. |
| **Paint** | See pinto. |
| **Palomino** | A gold colored horse with blond or white mane and tail. |
| **Pastern** | The area between the hoof and fetlock joint on all four legs. |
| **Pelham bit** | A bit that include a chain that goes under the chin. Two sets of reins are used with this bit. |
| **Pigeon-toed** | A conformational fault in which the hooves are turned in towards each other. |
| **Pinto** | A color of horse. Large patches of brown or black and white. Also called a paint. |
| **Points** | Mane, tail, and lower legs. Sometimes includes the nuzzle. |
| **Pommel** | The foremost section of a saddle that fits over the withers. In a Western saddle, this is the "horn" which the rider can rest his hands on. |
| **Pony** | A full grown horse that is 14.2 hands or under. |
| **Rearing** | A vice in which the horse stands on his hind legs with both forelegs in the air, usually to unsettle a rider or rid himself of irritating tack. |

| | |
|---|---|
| **Registry** | The breeding organization in which a horse has registration papers. |
| **Reining** | A Western style of riding demonstrating tremendous agility in turning, stopping, lead changing and more. |
| **Roan** | A color of horse that has white hairs mixed with black (blue roan), bay (red roan),or chestnut (strawberry roan). |
| **Sire** | The father of a horse. |
| **Snaffle bit** | A simple bit, consisting of one bar or two bars linked in the middle. Rings at each end attach to the reins. Usually used in English riding styles. |
| **Snip** | a white marking between the nostrils |
| **Sock** | white extending up to the fetlock |
| **Spavin** | A bone enlargement of the hock resulting in lameness in one or two hind legs. |
| **Splay-footed** | A conformational fault in which the hooves are turned away from each other. |
| **Stallion** | A male horse that has not been gelded. |
| **Star** | any white marking above or between the eyes |
| **Stocking** | white extending up to the cannon |
| **Stripe** | a narrow white stripe down the face |
| **Stud** | A stallion that is kept for breeding purposes. |
| **Thoroughbred** | A breed of horse, said to be descended from 3 Arab stallions brought to Britain in the 17th century. Thoroughbreds average 16 hands. Most racehorses are thoroughbreds. Thoroughbreds make excellent hunter/jumpers . |
| **Trot** | One of the four gaits of a horse. One foreleg and the opposite hindleg are on the ground as the other foreleg and opposite hindleg are moving forward. This is faster than a walk but slower than a canter or gallop. |
| **Twitch** | A metal clasper applied to the top lip that is used to temporarily restrain a horse, usually for medical treatment. |

**Vetting a horse**   Paying a vet to examine a horse to provide a report on his health and soundness. A horse is said to have "vetted" if the vet returns a report of good health.

**Walleye**   An eye that has no pigment or a blue tint. Vision is not affected by the color of the iris.

**Western**   A style of riding that includes many sports such as reining, roping, pleasure, trail and cutting. Characterized by the cowboy style saddle with a large pommel. The rider holds both reins with one hand, and steers the horse moving both reins towards the direction of the turn.

**Withers**   The slight ridge in a horse's back just before the mane starts. This is where height is measured on a horse.

# INDEX

mustang, 104

training, 5, 12, 22, 23, 27, 58, 75,
    80, 83, 94, 97, 101, 109, 111,
    113, 123, 124, 125, 129, 130,
    170, 171, 172
turning out, 60

# —U—

U.S. Dressage Team, 170
U.S. Equestrian Team, 170
*Understanding Your Horse's Health*,
    177
United Stated Dressage Federation,
    175
United States Combined Training
    Association, 175
United States Equestrian Team, 176
United States Pony Clubs, 176

# —V—

vet, 34, 39, 41, 51, 56, 59, 69, 70,
    71, 83, 87, 101, 108, 113, 115,
    116, 121, 142, 143, 148, 149,
    154, 158, 161
    costs, 84
videos, 137

# —W—

waste
    disposal, 66
watering, 43
way of going, 129
Western, 12, 20, 75, 104, 123, 130,
    133, 171, 172

Western Horse, The, 172
Western Horseman, 172
*Wild Horse\, The*
    *An Adopter's Manual*, 105
Wild Horse: An Adopter's Manual,
    The, 177
wild horses, 39, 104
worming, 70

# —Z—

zoning ordinances, 36

## Order Form

To order additional copies of *Buying Your First Horse* :

Company Name:_____

Name:_____

Address:_____

City:_____St:_____Zip:_____


_____books @ $16.95 per book _____

If shipping to Georgia add 5%_____

Shipping costs  $4.00 per order_____

Total_____

Send check or money order to:

White Papers Press
P.O. Box 72294-0
Marietta, GA  30007-2294


Your feedback is welcomed and appreciated.  Please write the above address or Email WPP@juno.com.

## Order Form

To order additional copies of *Buying Your First Horse* :

Company Name:_____
Name:_____
Address:_____
City:_____St:_____Zip:_____


_____books @ $16.95 per book _____
If shipping to Georgia add 5%_____
Shipping costs $4.00 per order_____
Total_____

Send check or money order to:

White Papers Press
P.O. Box 72294-0
Marietta, GA  30007-2294

Your feedback is welcomed and appreciated.  Please write the above address or Email WPP@juno.com.